SOLVE IT YOURSELF
MYSTERIES

Designer: Joe Pedley
Photographer: Sue Atkinson
Series Editor: Gaby Waters

AN IMPORTANT MESSAGE TO THE READER

I need your help urgently. The hat down by the map belongs to Sam Goodhorn, sheriff of the frontier town of Morgan's Gulch. The hole in it came from a bullet fired from a revolver made by the Sharpe Gun & Locksmith Company of Harpersville. The bullet went clean through the hat: in one side and out the other.

Fortunately, the sheriff had the hat in his hand at the time . . . and not on his head. He wasn't so lucky with the next shot. It caught him in the leg. He was shot at from behind so didn't see who fired the gun. The sheriff is in a bad way over at the hospital in Fort Granger. The only witness was a dog called Jake, and he's not saying much.

Your mission is to visit Morgan's Gulch to try to find out **WHO SHOT THE SHERIFF**. In the words of Deputy Williams, 'You gotta get to the bottom of things'.

Good luck, and watch your back.

Hank Stickleback

Hank Stickleback
State Governor

P.S. I've booked you a room at the Silver Dollar Saloon.

Delivered by Hand. August 1891.

Written
by
Phil Roxbee Cox

Photography
by
Sue Atkinson

Designed
by
Joe Pedley

Project
Co-ordinated
by Rupert Heath

Series
Editor:
Gaby Waters

By the time you reach page 41, you should be able to point your finger at the culprit. There are clues lurking throughout the story, and questions to be answered to help you on your way. But, to say who shot the sheriff, you'll need to make your own deductions and use your best powers of reasoning. This is real detective work. You'll need to fill in the gaps.

If you get stuck, you'll find some helpful hints on page 42. The answers are on pages 43 to 47. You'll find the solution to the whole mystery on page 48.

MORGAN'S GULCH Main Street

Corral Blacksmiths Silver Dollar Saloon General Store TO HOUSES

Railroad Station

M A I N   S T R E E T

Telegraph Office Sheriff's Office & Jailhouse Grimcheek's Undertakers Doc Wesley's Barbershop Clothing & Tailoring Store

GO SEE DEATH VALLEY.
ONE VISIT AND YOU'LL NEVER GO ANYWHERE ELSE

SAM SADDLER'S SADDLES
SADDLE UP AND RIDE OFF IN LESS THAN AN HOUR.
FOR ALL YOUR LEATHER REQUIREMENTS VISIT SAM'S
HIGH STREET, PERSVILLE

CHAPS! CHAPS! CHAPS!
And not just chaps.
When it comes to cowboy & cowgirl clothing, visit Morgan's Gulch clothing and clothing store

BLACKSMITH

MARTIN SPLODGE PRINTING CO.
Professional printers
THREE LETTER STYLES
CHOOSE FROM

I'VE SEEN THE LIONS OF B.J.BALHAM'S CIRCUS

TOMAHAWKS SHARPENED, ARROWS RE-SUCKERED BY 'POINTY PETE' OF THE FLEET-OF-FOOT TRIBE

DOC WESLEY.
HAIRCUTS, SHAVES, BEARD TRIMS & TOOTH PULLING.
MORGAN'S GULCH.

STAGECOACH TO MORGAN'S GULCH

Time: Wednesday, 18th of August, 1891, 12:25pm
Place: Morgan's Gulch, Main Street, facing
the sheriff's office

You arrive at the town of Morgan's Gulch on the
noon stagecoach (which is late) and help the only
other passenger, a preacher, down with his luggage.
The place is dusty, that's for sure. Dusty and hot.
It's time to check into your room.

Where are you staying? How do you get there?

I bought my spurs from HANK STALLION ACCESSORIES Harpersville.

NEARLY-NEW WHEELS AT

DESERT MIRAGE OIL for shiny, healthy e

This is to certify that
Clint & Betsy Gold of *The Silver Dollar Saloon*
are licensed, by law, to sell
OLDE SOCKS, DYN-O-MITE and
SCORPION'S TAIL
for one year, up until 31st of July, 1891
after which this permit must be renewed.

By order of Sheriff Goodhorn
Penalty for failing to renew: $2,000

DYN-O-MITE
THE TASTE OF
STRAWBERRIES
WITH THE KICK OF
A MULE.
J.T.MONROE
INDUSTRIES

SCORPION'S
TAIL
Stingingly
strong with a
surprise in
every bottle

OLDE SOCKS
THE INKY BLUE
DRINK
WITH A TANG OF
STEWED CHEESE.

RAT POISON
KEEP
LOCKED
AWAY

THE SILVER DOLLAR SALOON

Time: Wednesday, 12:33pm
Place: In the bar of *The Silver Dollar Saloon*

You stride into the saloon where you'll be staying for the next few days. The piano player stops mid-tune. Up at the bar you order a Rattlesnake Shake. Clint, the landlord, glares at you. "Have you been sent to find out who shot the sheriff ?" he asks. You nod. "We're better off without him," he says.

Why might Clint feel that?

JAILHOUSE BLUES

Time: Wednesday, 1:02pm
Place: Sheriff's office inside the jailhouse

With your luggage at the saloon, it's time to meet Deputy Williams. He isn't wearing a gun. "Sheriff's orders," he tells you, his feet up on the desk. "He's never let anybody carry a gun in this town." He points to a revolver. "He was shot with this one. The sheriff took it off Doc Wesley the day before he was shot, and left it on this here desk."

Doc Wesley? Who's he?

RULE BOOK

Marked cards

Doc Wesley's gun

Fool's gold

Loaded dice

ARREST WARRANTS

CONFISCATIONS BOOK

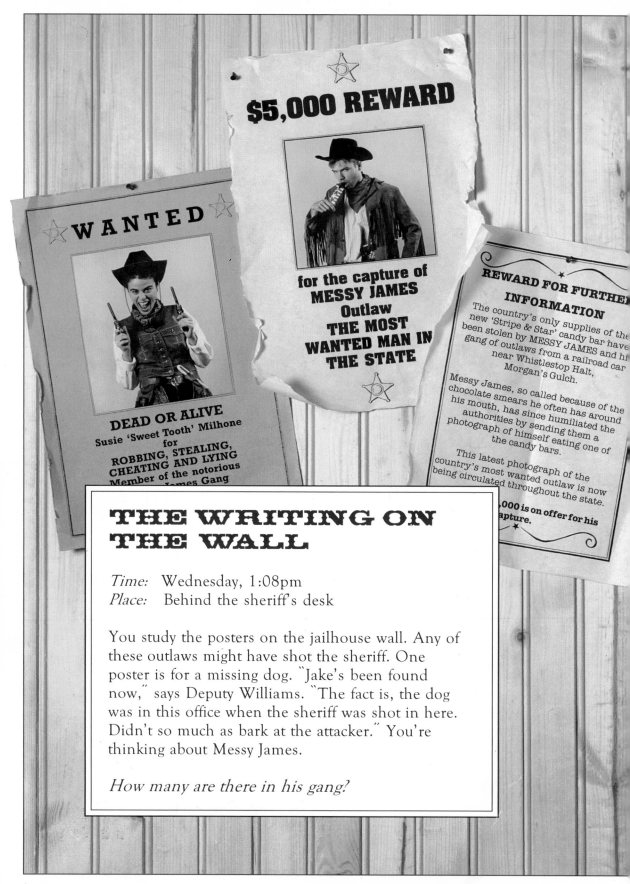

$5,000 REWARD

for the capture of
MESSY JAMES
Outlaw
THE MOST
WANTED MAN IN
THE STATE

W A N T E D

DEAD OR ALIVE
Susie 'Sweet Tooth' Milhone
for
ROBBING, STEALING,
CHEATING AND LYING
Member of the notorious
~~James Gang~~

REWARD FOR FURTHER
INFORMATION

The country's only supplies of the
new 'Stripe & Star' candy bar have
been stolen by MESSY JAMES and his
gang of outlaws from a railroad car
near Whistlestop Halt,
Morgan's Gulch.

Messy James, so called because of the
chocolate smears he often has around
his mouth, has since humiliated the
authorities by sending them a
photograph of himself eating one of
the candy bars.

This latest photograph of the
country's most wanted outlaw is now
being circulated throughout the state.

,000 is on offer for his
apture.

THE WRITING ON THE WALL

Time: Wednesday, 1:08pm
Place: Behind the sheriff's desk

You study the posters on the jailhouse wall. Any of these outlaws might have shot the sheriff. One poster is for a missing dog. "Jake's been found now," says Deputy Williams. "The fact is, the dog was in this office when the sheriff was shot in here. Didn't so much as bark at the attacker." You're thinking about Messy James.

How many are there in his gang?

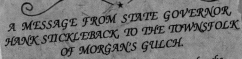

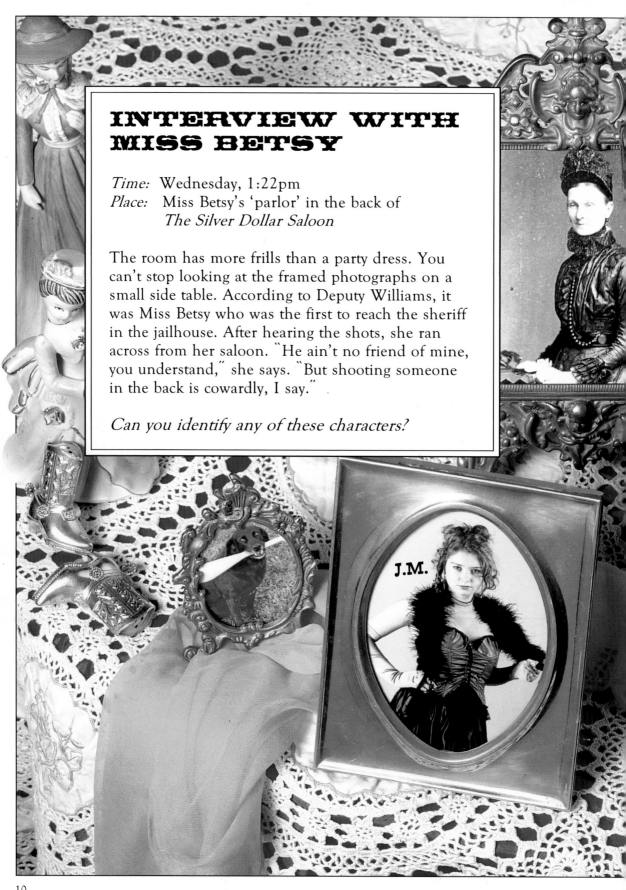

INTERVIEW WITH MISS BETSY

Time: Wednesday, 1:22pm
Place: Miss Betsy's 'parlor' in the back of
The Silver Dollar Saloon

The room has more frills than a party dress. You can't stop looking at the framed photographs on a small side table. According to Deputy Williams, it was Miss Betsy who was the first to reach the sheriff in the jailhouse. After hearing the shots, she ran across from her saloon. "He ain't no friend of mine, you understand," she says. "But shooting someone in the back is cowardly, I say."

Can you identify any of these characters?

J.M.

To Miss Betsy
With Best
Wishes
Doc Wesley

A HALF DOLLAR HAIRCUT

Time: Wednesday, 3:15pm
Place: Doc Wesley's tooth pulling and barbershop

It's time to speak to the man whose revolver was used to shoot the sheriff. You sit in Doc Wesley's barber's chair and stare into his wall cabinet. "Goodhorn took the gun off me the day before the shootin'," says the Doc. "Okay, so it has a hair trigger and sometimes goes off by accident when you pick it up . . . but the sheriff had no right to take it. He's never liked me seeing as how I'm new to these parts."

Interesting. How long has he had this shop?

AN ANONYMOUS TIP-OFF

Time: Wednesday, 7:08pm
Place: Your bedroom, *The Silver Dollar Saloon*

After a hard day of investigating, you're ready to read in bed. A message wrapped around a rock has just sailed through your bedroom window and landed on the quilt with a crash. It was lucky that the message didn't hit you on arrival, or you'd be in no fit state to read anything.

What does the message say?

OAOLOO ONOEII
OEONOO OCOLOO OCOROC OOOMOE
OTOAOK OEOROS OAOTOE OLOEOV
OMOEOI ONOTOH OEOUN ODEOR
OOOPOT OOOTOH OEOMOM OEOEOT
OWOAON OTOTOO OPOUOT OAOSOT
OOOUON OOTOO OWONOA ONOUON
OEOION OGOSOP OROEOA ONODOI
OHOEOR OEOAOR OEOEOA ODOAOR
OIOFOP OGOOOO OEOLOI OEOSOB
OOOOOT OIONOG OOOFOS OHOEOR
OOOUOA OBOOOU OOOFOS ORONOT
OIOMOU OSOTOT OAOLOK OTOO OY

...N'S GULCH NEWS

...SSY JAMES GANG ...RIKES AGAIN!

...and outlaws correspondent

...e turning from bad to ...Gulch. Many people ...o criticize Sheriff ...ctly following of ...it comes to his ...mes gang, the ...d and clear.

...n.

...e of men ...n these ...t that ...wn

TROUBLE BREWING IN ELBOW CREEK

from our troublesome correspondent

There's nothing like a touch of gold fever to cause disputes, disagreements and fistfights over who owns what land. That's exactly what's happened in Elbow Creek since the discovery of gold in Elbow River.

"By rights that land belongs to the Fleet-of-Foot tribe," says Sheriff Goodhorn of Morgan's Gulch, "but there are some bad folks who claim otherwise."

Tomorrow's Morgan's Gulch News will carry a full report.

MISS ALICIA MONROE RETURNS TO COUNTY

from our social scene editor

Miss Alicia Monroe, beautiful daughter of Beef Baron and cattle king J.T. Monroe, has returned to live at the family homestead.

Instantly recognizable with a beauty spot on her cheek and her famous bull's skull ring, Miss Alicia told me: "Bright city lights not for me. I'm a humble country girl at heart." When asked about local ...is to marr... Hopi...

 TO THE UNDERTAKER'S

Time: Wednesday, 11:07pm
Place: Carpentry room, the Undertaker's

Following the instructions in the message, you find yourself in a room of half-made coffins. You catch sight of a man in the shadows. "I'm Mort Grimcheek," he whispers. "Whatever you've heard, I didn't shoot the sheriff. The talk is that I want more guns around because more guns mean more deaths, an' more deaths mean more business for me. But it ain't true." There's something not quite right about the undertaker.

What is it?

IMPRESSIONS

Time: Wednesday, 11:14pm
Place: Outside the Undertaker's

You follow the fake Mort Grimcheek outside but he's up on his horse and away before you can shout 'imposter!' A huge lizard lumbers past. From the light of a window above, you search the ground for clues . . . a footprint . . . hoof prints . . . *anything* that might confirm who the man in the shadows really was. The candy bar wrapper's a giveaway.

Why?

ON THE TRACK

Time: Thursday, 10:26am
Place: On a steam train bound for *Whistlestop Halt*

A sunny morning. The girl in the train seat opposite you has her face half-hidden by a fan. She looks nervous. Following a lead, you're told that the real Mort Grimcheek is out of town . . . and that someone who really *hates* the sheriff is Jonah Johnson. You're on your way to visit him along the stretch of the Elbow River where he pans for gold. You look back at the girl.

Any clues as to who she could be?

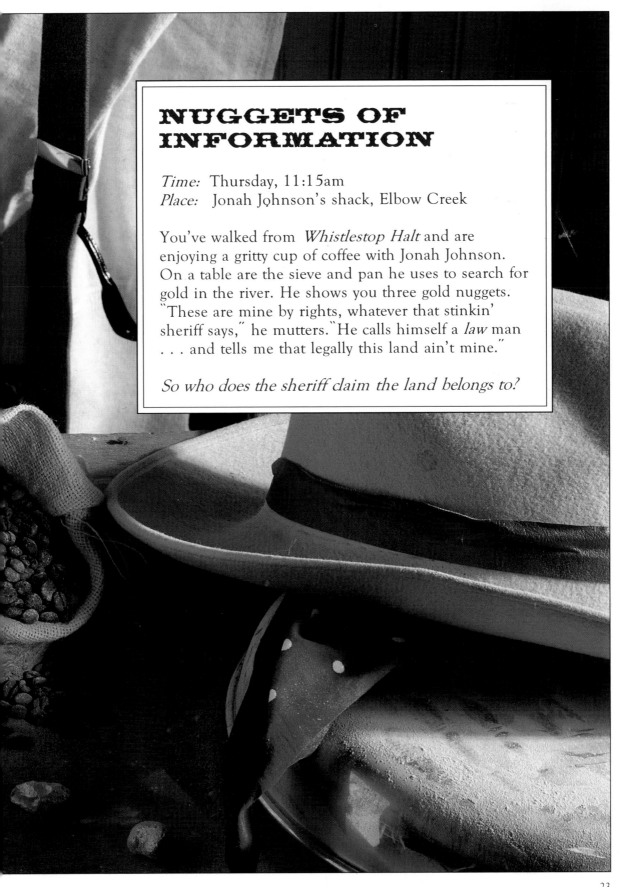

NUGGETS OF INFORMATION

Time: Thursday, 11:15am
Place: Jonah Johnson's shack, Elbow Creek

You've walked from *Whistlestop Halt* and are enjoying a gritty cup of coffee with Jonah Johnson. On a table are the sieve and pan he uses to search for gold in the river. He shows you three gold nuggets. "These are mine by rights, whatever that stinkin' sheriff says," he mutters. "He calls himself a *law* man . . . and tells me that legally this land ain't mine."

So who does the sheriff claim the land belongs to?

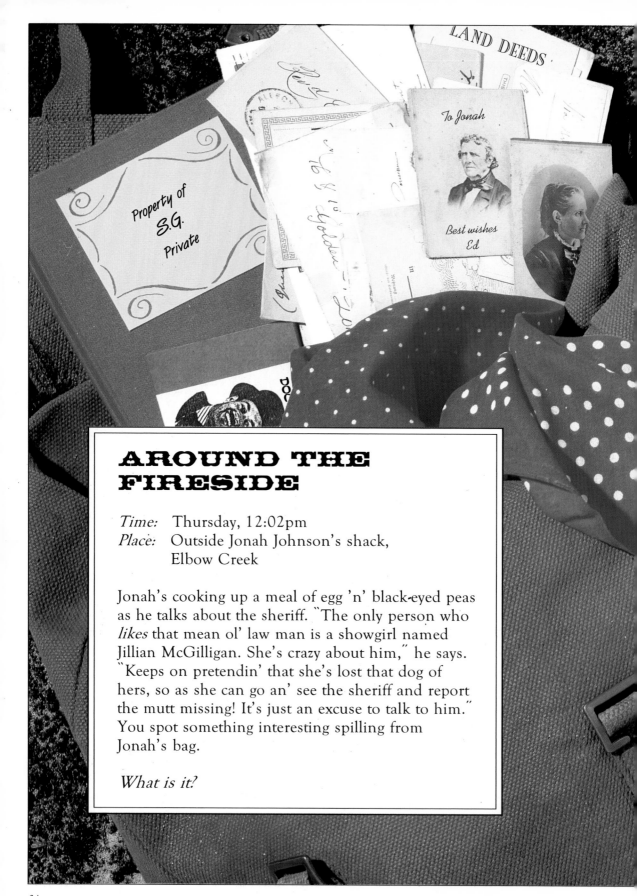

AROUND THE FIRESIDE

Time: Thursday, 12:02pm
Place: Outside Jonah Johnson's shack,
Elbow Creek

Jonah's cooking up a meal of egg 'n' black-eyed peas
as he talks about the sheriff. "The only person who
likes that mean ol' law man is a showgirl named
Jillian McGilligan. She's crazy about him," he says.
"Keeps on pretendin' that she's lost that dog of
hers, so as she can go an' see the sheriff and report
the mutt missing! It's just an excuse to talk to him."
You spot something interesting spilling from
Jonah's bag.

What is it?

The people of Morgan's Gulch are becoming more lawless by the day. No wonder that gutless Sheriff Meacher upped and left the town a year ago, leaving me the silver star of office and the job of upholding law and order.

Last Wednesday, I saw Max Henkle leave the general store and drop a piece of twine on the ground. When I threatened him with a dollar fine for such disgraceful littering, he said 'Sorry' as though that would make things better. This sloppiness could lead to open rebellion on the streets.

I need a firmer hand.

As for Deputy Williams, I reckon he's after my job. Fat chance. He's more interested in his good looks than he is in keeping the bad element out of Morgan's Gulch – always admiring himself in the mirror and combing back his hair.

He spends more time in the barber's chair than he does behind his desk.

And as for all those quack doctors and medicine men, they're banned from Morgan's Gulch. I won't have a single one of them selling pills and potions in my town. No, sir.

BY THE BOOK

Time: Thursday, 12:35pm, after lunch
Place: Still outside Jonah's shack

Jonah is quick to point out that he'd simply *found* the sheriff's notebook. "I didn't wound him and take it off of him," he says. "He must've dropped it." You flick through the pages and soon see why Sheriff Goodhorn is such an unpopular man in and around the town of Morgan's Gulch. He's a stickler for every rule and regulation. "Even the town tailor don't like 'im," grins Jonah. "And *he's* friends with just about everyone."

Who is the tailor? What's he done wrong?

Fines still to be paid:

MA GRIFFIN . . . .
for failing to wear her false teeth in a public place $3.00

LOU MACFARLANE . . . .
for failing to raise his hat to Miss Betsy on Sunday $1.50

DIRK MULGREW . . . .
speaking with his mouth full   50c

BAD WITHERS . . . .
sneezing without a handkerchief in the bar $2.00

NE MARLDON . . . .
chewing gum on a Friday $3.00

Y NORTON . . . .
overcharging senior citizens   50c

27

WAITING IN A TEEPEE

Time: Thursday, 2:45pm
Place: Inside a teepee of the Fleet-of-Foot tribe

You sit staring at the rug-covered floor, waiting to see if Chief Peacemaker will agree to talk to you. You found his name in the sheriff's notebook and borrowed Jonah's mule to ride out here to the tribe's settlement. Something catches your eye that suggests that the chief's braves are doing more in Elbow River than just hunting and fishing.

What is it?

have been making the
Our most popular revol
the Sharpe-Shooter.45
is now av
black revo
chamber and butt grip.
For further information,
ot visit our
persville showroom or speak
e of our
local agents?

A POWWOW WITH THE CHIEF

Time: Thursday, 3:15pm
Place: Chief Peacemaker's teepee

From the way they treat his picture, you reckon that Sheriff Goodhorn isn't too popular around these parts. But did one of the Fleet-of-Foot's braves actually shoot him? "Goodhorn does not like people carrying guns and neither do I," says Chief Peacemaker. "My braves have no interest in white men's weapons," he says. "We hunt with spears and arrows."

Do you believe him?

MEDICINE MAN

Time: Thursday, 3:22pm
Place: In the middle of the Fleet-of-Foot's settlement

Just as you were expected to smoke a pipe of peace, a clattering of wheels brought everyone outside – and face to face with Doctor Theopolis J. Canard and his 'MEDICINE SHOW'. You study his bottles and boxes of potions and pills. "Step right up!" he cries. "Time is short and I'm on my way to Morgan's Gulch. I've got pills to keep you awake and potions to help you sleep. Now, what'll it be? Don't be shy! Step right up!"

Where have you seen his face before?
Why might he be another suspect?

DOCTOR CANARD'S
Perfect
Pick Me Up
Potion

DOCTOR
CANARD'S
Enlivening
Lip Lotion

DOCTOR CANARD'
Glorious
Throat
Gargler

DOCTOR CANARD'S
Fantastic
Foot Swamp
Soother

DOCTOR CANARD'S
Amazing
Wrinkle
Remover

DOCTOR CANARD'S
Marvelo
Mou
Freshen

DOCTOR CANARD'S
Tested
Tiredness
Tablets

DOCTOR CANARD'S
Hearty
Headache
Healers

DOCTOR CANARD'S
Comfy Kidney
Pills
Take two daily

DOCTOR C
S

DOCTOR

Wednesday.
Don't forget to visit C.P. about
possibility of purchases.

J. T. MONROE INDUSTRIES
Founder & President J.T. Monroe
Offices worldwide.

Order more
DYN-O-MITE

Hank Stickleback

Hank Stickleback
State Governor

splattered like a broken melon.
As for the other matter you asked me to look into,
J.T., I'm afraid that Sam Goodhorn is unwilling to
see things our way. He has stated that you 'may own
most of this county and half of the state', but you'll
never own him. According to him, even the richest
~son isn't above the law." I have tried to
~l to F. L. about ~

BACK AT THE RANCH

Time: Thursday, 6:11pm
Place: The study, inside J.T. Monroe's ranch

One mule ride, train journey and brisk walk later,
you're looking through the desk of J.T. Monroe.
He's one man you can't afford to miss on a visit to
Morgan's Gulch. He owns most of the land and *all*
of the cattle for miles around, and should be worth
talking to. His servant told you to wait in here, but
you're having a quick look around.

Any useful information here?

THE CATTLE KING

Time: Thursday, 7:00pm on the dot
Place: J.T. Monroe's stables

You're finally taken out to meet the great man. He doesn't look like a millionaire. He looks more like a cowboy, from the Stetson on his head down to those cowboy boots of his you're admiring. "Sheriff Goodhorn's a little law man who's too big for his britches," says J.T. "But I didn't have him shot." Local talk, however, is that J.T. is selling guns to the Fleet-of-Foot tribe.

Any clues that he's been to see them?

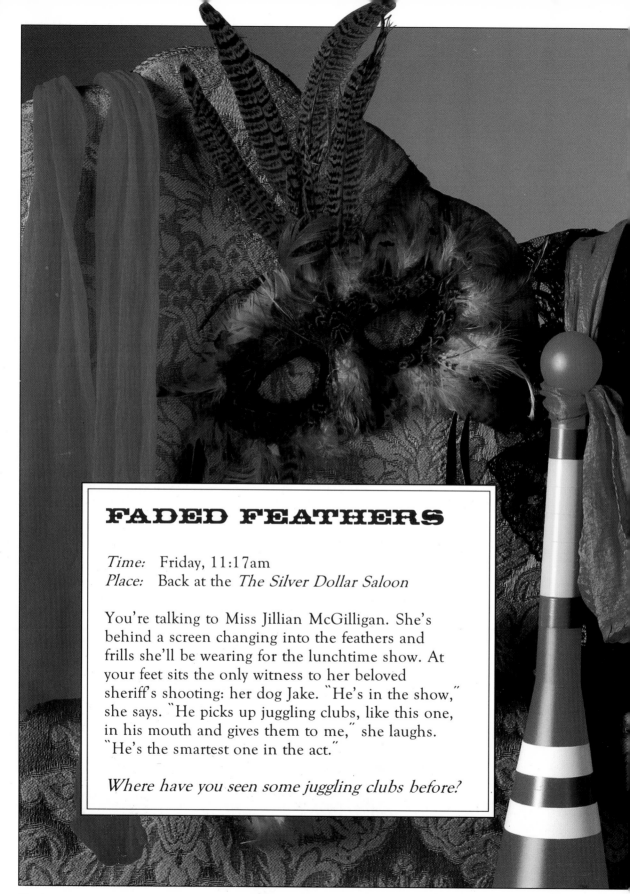

FADED FEATHERS

Time:　Friday, 11:17am
Place:　Back at the *The Silver Dollar Saloon*

You're talking to Miss Jillian McGilligan. She's behind a screen changing into the feathers and frills she'll be wearing for the lunchtime show. At your feet sits the only witness to her beloved sheriff's shooting: her dog Jake. "He's in the show," she says. "He picks up juggling clubs, like this one, in his mouth and gives them to me," she laughs. "He's the smartest one in the act."

Where have you seen some juggling clubs before?

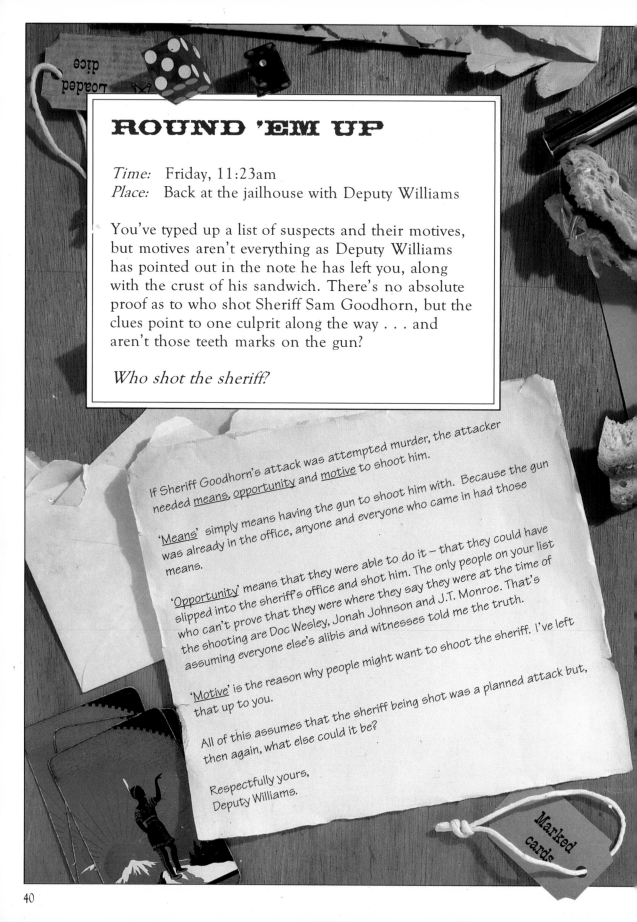

ROUND 'EM UP

Time: Friday, 11:23am
Place: Back at the jailhouse with Deputy Williams

You've typed up a list of suspects and their motives, but motives aren't everything as Deputy Williams has pointed out in the note he has left you, along with the crust of his sandwich. There's no absolute proof as to who shot Sheriff Sam Goodhorn, but the clues point to one culprit along the way . . . and aren't those teeth marks on the gun?

Who shot the sheriff?

If Sheriff Goodhorn's attack was attempted murder, the attacker needed <u>means</u>, <u>opportunity</u> and <u>motive</u> to shoot him.

'<u>Means</u>' simply means having the gun to shoot him with. Because the gun was already in the office, anyone and everyone who came in had those means.

'<u>Opportunity</u>' means that they were able to do it – that they could have slipped into the sheriff's office and shot him. The only people on your list who can't prove that they were where they say they were at the time of the shooting are Doc Wesley, Jonah Johnson and J.T. Monroe. That's assuming everyone else's alibis and witnesses told me the truth.

'<u>Motive</u>' is the reason why people might want to shoot the sheriff. I've left that up to you.

All of this assumes that the sheriff being shot was a planned attack but, then again, what else could it be?

Respectfully yours,
Deputy Williams.

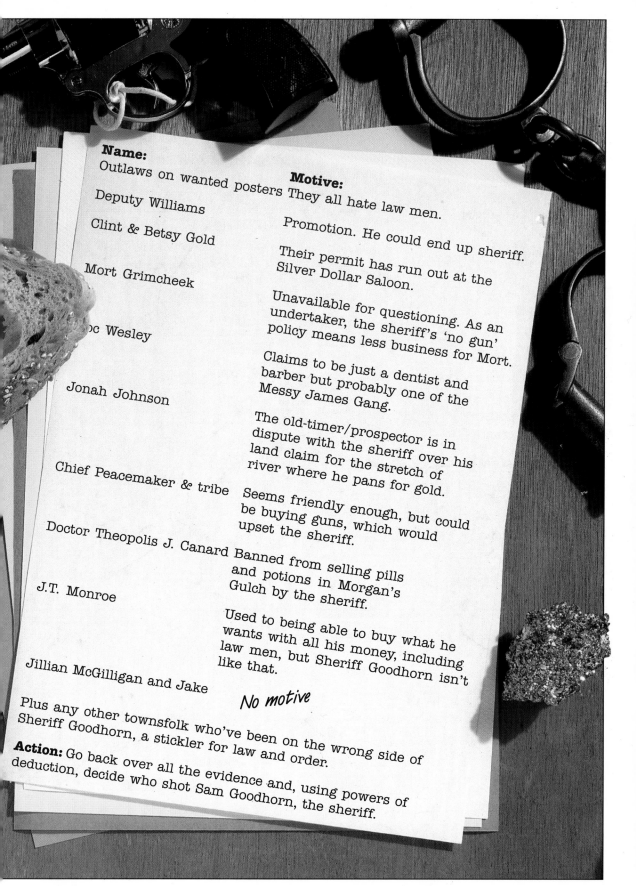

Name:	Motive:
Outlaws on wanted posters	They all hate law men.
Deputy Williams	Promotion. He could end up sheriff.
Clint & Betsy Gold	Their permit has run out at the Silver Dollar Saloon.
Mort Grimcheek	Unavailable for questioning. As an undertaker, the sheriff's 'no gun' policy means less business for Mort.
oc Wesley	Claims to be just a dentist and barber but probably one of the Messy James Gang.
Jonah Johnson	The old-timer/prospector is in dispute with the sheriff over his land claim for the stretch of river where he pans for gold.
Chief Peacemaker & tribe	Seems friendly enough, but could be buying guns, which would upset the sheriff.
Doctor Theopolis J. Canard	Banned from selling pills and potions in Morgan's Gulch by the sheriff.
J.T. Monroe	Used to being able to buy what he wants with all his money, including law men, but Sheriff Goodhorn isn't like that.
Jillian McGilligan and Jake	*No motive*

Plus any other townsfolk who've been on the wrong side of Sheriff Goodhorn, a stickler for law and order.

Action: Go back over all the evidence and, using powers of deduction, decide who shot Sam Goodhorn, the sheriff.

HELPFUL HINTS

PAGES 2 & 3
Hank Stickleback can help you here.

PAGES 4 & 5
It's the sheriff's duty to make sure that everything is up to date.

PAGES 6 & 7
The answer lies on someone's luggage.

PAGES 8 & 9
The answer's in the small print. Read it carefully.

PAGES 10 & 11
The posters on the sheriff's wall should help you identify *three* characters.

PAGES 12 & 13
His card says he's been in Morgan's Gulch 'since 1890'. What year is this investigation taking place?

PAGES 14 & 15
Oooo? I don't think they're all necessary.

PAGES 16 & 17
Isn't there something about Mort on the sheriff's office wall? There are some pictures of some very nasty characters there too.

PAGES 18 & 19
The candy should wrap this riddle up.

PAGES 20 & 21
Perhaps she's been mentioned in the newspapers.

PAGES 22 & 23
Look at your bedtime reading matter again.

PAGES 24 & 25
It belongs to the sheriff.

PAGES 26 & 27
The tailor has been named somewhere before. Match this name with one of the names here.

PAGES 28 & 29
There's an object here similar to something Jonah Johnson has back in his hut.

PAGES 30 & 31
The answer lies in the other teepee.

PAGES 32 & 33
Is he a friend of Miss Betsy's? And doesn't Jonah take his pills? As for why he might be a suspect, what does the sheriff have to say about quack doctors?

PAGES 34 & 35
Something on J.T.Monroe's desk is revealing about his attitude to lawmen.

PAGES 36 & 37
A boot could hold a clue . . . or not.

PAGES 38 & 39
You've seen two. One in black and white, and one very near the beginning of your investigation.

PAGES 40 & 41
Go back over all the evidence . . .

ANSWERS

PAGES 2 & 3
According to Governor Hank Stickleback's letter on page 1, he's booked you a room at the *Silver Dollar Saloon* – so that's where you should be going next. You can find out where it is in **Main Street** by studying the map he gave you.

PAGES 4 & 5
On the bar are bottles of **DYN-O-MITE**, **SCORPION'S TAIL** and **OLDE SOCKS**. According to the permit behind Clint's shoulder, these can't be sold without an up-to-date permit. This one ran out on 31st of July, 1891 . . . and Hank Stickleback didn't send you his letter until August. With the sheriff out of the way, it looks as if Clint hasn't bothered to buy a new permit. He can sell the drinks illegally.

PAGES 6 & 7
Doc Wesley's name appears on one of the labels on the preacher's trunk that you helped to get down from the stagecoach on pages 2 & 3. It says that he does 'HAIRCUTS, SHAVES, BEARD TRIMMING AND TOOTH PULLING' in Morgan's Gulch. That makes him the local barber and tooth-puller . . . not the most popular job in town!

PAGES 8 & 9
According to the poster headed '*A MESSAGE FROM STATE GOVERNOR . . .*', Messy James and '*his evil gang of twelve*' were involved in a recent robbery . . . so there are thirteen of them, including Messy himself!

PAGES 10 & 11

There are three 'familiar' characters who can be identified in Miss Betsy's photographs. The most obvious is probably Doc Wesley. He's signed his photo . . . but there's something else about him that could be important. According to the '**HAVE YOU SEEN**' poster on pages 8 & 9, the hunt is on for '**A man with a v-shaped scar on his right cheek, believed to be a retired & reformed member of the Messy James gang**'. Doesn't he have such a scar?

Jake the dog is also easy to spot. There's another picture of him on a **WANTED** poster on the jailhouse wall on pages 8 & 9. In the description, he's described as being part of Miss Jillian McGilligan's '**animal juggling act**'.

The woman in the photo next to Jake is dressed as a showgirl and has the initials **J.M.** on her photo. It's more than likely, then, that's she's Jake's owner, Miss Jillian McGilligan '**of the Silver Dollar Saloon**'.

PAGES 12 & 13

According to Doc Wesley's card, on the righthand door of his cabinet, he's been 'Hairdresser & Toothpuller in Morgan's Gulch since 1890'. According to the date on Hank Stickleback's letter (and the date under 'Time' on pages 2 & 3), it's now August 1891. That means that the Doc's been in business here from anything between 9 months and almost 18 months. This could tie in with him being a recently retired outlaw.

PAGES 14 & 15

The message tied to the rock thrown through your bedroom window may look like it's in a difficult code, but it's easy to read once you've cracked it. There's a letter 'o' in front of each and every letter. All the letters have been divided into groups of six. Simply remove the extra 'o's, divide the remaining letters into words, add punctuation and the message reads:

I MUST TALK TO YOU ABOUT THE SHOOTING OF SHERIFF GOODHORN THERE ARE LIES BEING SPREAD AROUND TOWN AND I WANT TO PUT A STOP TO THEM. MEET ME IN THE UNDERTAKERS AT ELEVEN O' CLOCK. COME ALONE!!

PAGES 16 & 17

The real Mort Grimcheek, undertaker, wears an eyepatch. In the ' *MESSAGE TO THE PEOPLE OF MORGAN'S GULCH* ' on pages 8 & 9, the State Governor gives special praise to Mr. Grimcheek for losing his eye *'when attempting to topple James from his horse'*. This man has two eyes . . . and looks suspiciously like Messy James, photographed on the wanted poster in the sheriff's office.

PAGES 18 & 19

The dropped wrapper looks like the 'Stripe & Star' candy bar being held by Messy James in the poster on page 8. According to that poster 'the country's only supplies of the new 'Stripe & Star' candy bar have been stolen by MESSY JAMES and his gang.' This further adds to the evidence that the man you've been talking to is Messy James himself.

PAGES 20 & 21

An article in **MORGAN'S GULCH NEWS**, in your room at the Silver Dollar Saloon on pages 14 & 15, describes J.T. Monroe's daughter, Alicia, as being 'instantly recognizable with a beauty spot on her cheek and a bull's skull ring on her finger.' The woman opposite you on the train has both the beauty spot and the ring. It's therefore likely that she's Miss Alicia Monroe.

PAGES 22 & 23

The answer once again lies in the newspaper on pages 14 & 15, but in a different article. Under the heading **'TROUBLE BREWING IN ELBOW CREEK'**, the sheriff is quoted as saying: 'By rights that land belongs to the Fleet-of-Foot tribe.'

PAGES 24 & 25

There seem to be a number of interesting items sticking out of the old-timer's bag, but the most curious must be the book marked '*Property of S. G. Private.*' S. G. are Sheriff Sam Goodhorn's initials. This must be his book.

PAGES 26 & 27

The first step is to work out who the tailor is. For this you'll need to go back and look at the cards in Doc Wesley's barbershop on pages 12 & 13. Sure enough, one of the advertisements reads: 'SHANE MARLDON Town Tailor to Morgan's Gulch.' Now all you have to do is find the name in the sheriff's notebook. Marldon's crime is spelled out as: '*chewing gum on a Friday*'.

PAGES 28 & 29

Among the jumble of bows, arrows, tomahawks and spears lies a sieve which is almost identical to the one you saw on the table in Jonah Johnson's shack on pages 22 & 23. Jonah said that he used *his* to search for gold in Elbow River. This means that it's likely that the Fleet-of-Foot tribe are using *theirs* for a similar purpose. They're doing a little gold prospecting of their own.

PAGES 30 & 31

Although Chief Peacemaker says that his braves only hunt with spears and arrows, there is a leaflet for the 'Sharpe-Shooter.45' lying, half-covered, in the teepee you just left on pages 28 & 29. Perhaps he is more interested in 'white men's weapons' than he is letting on.

Interestingly, in his letter to you on page 1, Hank Stickleback describes the revolver used to shoot the sheriff being made by the '*Sharpe Gun & Locksmith Company*'. The gun in the leaflet is also described as having a '**golden finish**'. It seems likely that Doc Wesley's confiscated gun was, therefore, like the one in this leaflet: a Sharpe-Shooter .45.

PAGES 32 & 33

You've seen this face twice before. Once, on a packet of pills sticking out of the top of Jonah Johnson's bag when he was cooking up egg 'n' beans around the fire, on pages 24 & 25. Before that, in Miss Betsy's parlor on pages 10 & 11, there was a photograph of him raising his hat. Miss Betsy seems to have photos of plenty of strange characters . . .

And why might Doctor Canard have had reason to shoot the sheriff? In his notebook on pages 26 & 27, Sheriff Goodhorn wrote: '*As for all those quack doctors and medicine men, they're banned from Morgan's Gulch. I won't have a single one of them selling pills and potions in my town. No, sir.*' With the sheriff out of the way, Doctor Canard is now free to travel to the town. But would the doctor go so far as to shoot a person for that?

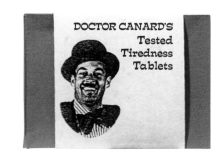

PAGES 34 & 35

There are a number of items that suggest J.T. Monroe might want the sheriff out of the way.

As his headed notepaper makes very clear, he is founder and president of J.T. MONROE INDUSTRIES. If you look at the label of the bottle of **DYN-O-MITE** on the bar on pages 4 & 5, you'll see that it's made by J.T. Monroe Industries . . . and if the Silver Dollar Saloon wasn't allowed to sell it any more because its permit has run out, J.T. would lose money.

Then there's the matter of the note on J.T's desk in which Sheriff Goodhorn is quoted as saying that J.T. *'may own most of this county and half of the state, but you'll never own [me].'* J.T. is the kind of man who would far rather have a lawman he could bribe.

PAGES 36 & 37

J.T. is only wearing a spur on one boot. The other spur must have fallen off somewhere. It has, and you've seen it . . . in Chief Peacemaker's teepee on pages 30 & 31. Not only that, sticking out of one of the drawers of J.T's desk, on pages 34 & 35, is the note: 'Don't forget to visit C.P. about possibility of purchases'. 'C.P.' could stand for Chief Peacemaker, and there was also that Sharpe Gun & Locksmith leaflet in the Fleet-of-Foot's wigwam. It seems probable that this talk of J.T. selling guns to the tribe is true.

PAGES 38 & 39

There was a juggling club in the mouth of Jake the dog in the photograph on Miss Betsy's table on pages 10 & 11, which isn't surprising considering his role in Miss Jillian McGilligan's act at the *Silver Dollar Saloon*.

There was also a (blue) juggling club on the sheriff's desk on page 6. Perhaps Jake had this in his mouth when he was found and taken to the sheriff's office on the day that Sheriff Goodhorn was shot.

PAGES 40 & 41

So you want to know who shot the sheriff? Well, you won't find the answer on this page. This is your last chance to decide who *you* think did it. Remember those words of advice on page 1: 'you'll need to make your own deductions and use your best powers of reasoning. This is real detective work. You'll need to fill in the gaps.' Ready? Then turn the page and hold it up against a mirror.

THE SOLUTION

The only living breathing creature known to be in the jailhouse with the sheriff at the time of the shooting was Jillian McGilligan's dog, Jake. According to Jonah Johnson on pages 24 & 25, Jillian "keeps on pretendin' that she's lost that dog of hers, just so as she can go and see the sheriff . . . She's crazy about him." Jake had been found and taken to the sheriff.

Jake likes holding things in his mouth. You can see him holding a juggling club in one of the photographs on Miss Betsy's table on pages 10 & 11. As Jillian McGilligan explained on pages 38 & 39, the dog was trained to pick up these juggling clubs in his mouth as a part of her performance. "He's the smartest one in the act," she said.

And what about the gun itself? A Sharpe .45, it belonged to Doc Wesley and was already on the sheriff's desk before the sheriff was shot. According to Deputy Williams on pages 4 & 5, "Sheriff Goodhorn took it off Doc Wesley the day before." On pages 12 & 13, Doc Wesley described the gun as having "a hair trigger and sometimes goes off by accident when you pick it up."

So let's look at the facts: the gun, that can go off by accident without the the trigger having to be pulled properly, is on a desk that also has a juggling club on it (see pages 6 & 7). The sheriff is shot in the lower back and in the hat that he's holding at his side . . . and the gun has teeth marks on its handle.

Jake the dog shot the sheriff. He had no idea what he was doing of course. He simply picked up the gun in his mouth (perhaps he was reaching for the blue juggling club) and it went off twice, shooting the poor old sheriff. No one is to blame. Except, perhaps, for Sheriff Goodhorn himself. He should have thought to take the bullets from the gun!

So the culprit was one of those shown on one of the wanted posters after all.

BY THE WAY . . .

Like any good detective, you're probably wondering why someone should pretend to be Mort Grimcheek the undertaker and act so suspiciously. The answer is simple. As you know, the man pretending to be Mort was none other than the outlaw Messy James himself. James was sure that he'd be Number One suspect for shooting the sheriff. By pretending to be Mort and protesting his innocence, he was actually trying to plant the idea in your mind that the undertaker had good reason for shooting Sheriff Goodhorn. It was a double bluff.

James picked on Mort Grimcheek to take the heat off himself, because Mort almost managed to capture him once. You can read about that in the poster on pages 8 & 9.

Reports have just come in that Sheriff Goodhorn is making a full recovery.

MONTGOMERY FANG
Professor of the Paranormal
Ghost 'n' Ghoul Hunter, Monster Catcher and
Ectoplasm Exterminator

Thursday, April 17

AN IMPORTANT WARNING TO THE READER

You are about to visit Razorback Hall, also known as the 'House of Horror'. Once the most haunted house in the country, Razorback Hall – ancestral home of the Rigsby family for over four centuries – has been free from ghosts for the past 75 years. Until a month ago, that is, when Sir Ralph became the master of the Hall.

Sir Ralph has instructed me to find out whether these new 'hauntings' are the work of genuine ghosts. There's always the possibility that they are some elaborate hoax. But for what purpose?

This is where you come in. I would take on the job myself, but I'm recovering from an attack of Swamp Fever, after tracking the infamous 'Bog Lady' to her lair . . . but that's another story.

You must go in my place. Spend this weekend at Razorback Hall and see if you can find out **WHO'S HAUNTING THE HOUSE OF HORROR** . . . the living or the dead. Apart from Sir Ralph himself, all living members of the Rigsby family should be there, as well as a Colonel Bloodheart, Claptrap the butler and Mrs. Stuffing the housekeeper.

Good luck!

Montgomery Fang

P.S. You're to sleep in the Mauve Room - once said to be the most haunted room in the whole house.

WRITTEN BY
RUPERT HEATH

DESIGNED BY
JOE PEDLEY

PHOTOGRAPHED BY
SUE ATKINSON

EDITED BY
PHIL ROXBEE COX

SERIES EDITOR
GABY WATERS

THERE ARE HELPFUL HINTS ON PAGE 90 AND THE ANSWERS ARE ON PAGES 91 TO 95. THE SOLUTION TO THE WHOLE MYSTERY IS ON PAGE 96.

ON ECTOPLASM –
MONTGOMERY FAM...

KEEPING FIT WHILE EXORCISING
BY
MON...
...G

SEMPER RIGSBIUS

Recent **RIGSBY FAMILY TREE**

Ebeneezer Rigsby (m. Carlotta Jones) - both deceased

Regina Rigsby (deceased) Zelda Rigsby Digory Rigsby (deceased) Jasper Rigsby (deceased?)
(m. Colonel W. Bloodheart) (m. Dorcas Smith (deceased))

Robin

Ralph

NOTES

- Relatives are shown in order of age - for example, Ebeneezer's daughter Regina is older than Zelda.
- A question mark hangs over the death of Jasper Rigsby, the explorer. A crocodile wearing Jasper's old school tie was found in the deepest jungle of Mazalaland. The family believe Jasper's final journey was down the croc's throat.
- Zelda Rigsby, once known as horror-movie star Selina Stromboli, lives in Razorback Hall with only Claptrap and Mrs. Stuffing for company. In he... old age she dabbles in the supernatural, believing she can see into the future.
- The Rigsby family tradition is for the eldest male blood relative to... inherit Razorback Hall.

PLACEBO
PILLS
FOR FAKE
ILLS

Sir Ralph
Rigsby

razorback hall
by robin rigsby
age 5

IN THE LAIR OF THE HUNTER

Time: 4pm, Thursday, April 17
Place: Professor Montgomery Fang's study

You've gone to tea with the Professor of the Paranormal in his cobweb-covered study. He doesn't look ill. 'Master Robin will drive you down to Razorback Hall tomorrow,' the Professor croaks, handing you piles of papers including a set of plans. 'Sir Ralph thinks these plans were lost,' he says, 'but they were found in a drawer at the Hall by the butler. Keep your wits about you when you're there. You'll need them!'

Is Sir Ralph the rightful owner of Razorback Hall? And who is this 'Master Robin'?

PLAN OF RAZORBACK HALL

Razorback Hall by Zelda Rigsby

I FOUGHT THE GORE (AND THE GORE WON)

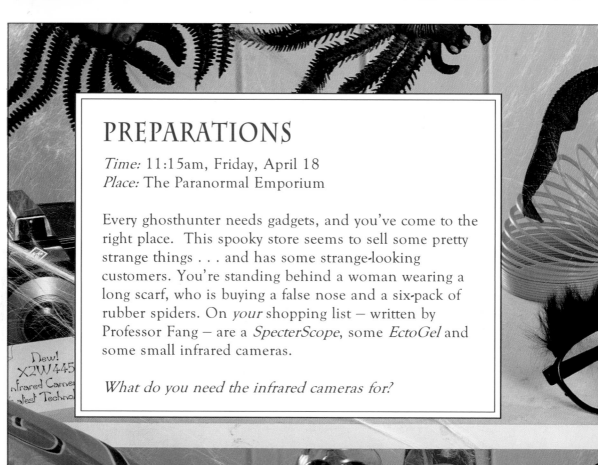

PREPARATIONS

Time: 11:15am, Friday, April 18
Place: The Paranormal Emporium

Every ghosthunter needs gadgets, and you've come to the right place. This spooky store seems to sell some pretty strange things . . . and has some strange-looking customers. You're standing behind a woman wearing a long scarf, who is buying a false nose and a six-pack of rubber spiders. On *your* shopping list — written by Professor Fang — are a *SpecterScope*, some *EctoGel* and some small infrared cameras.

What do you need the infrared cameras for?

The original!
Green gel turns purple
in the presence of the
paranormal

Magic Monster

Beans

Things get beastly
with a bellyful
of jelly!

Ectogel

Ectogel

TALON
TASTIES

Banish smooth
hands in a delicious
instant!

Just in!
Brings out the
beast in you!

BAT OIL
FLY 'N' FRY!

X2W339
Specterscope
Guaranteed performance.
Bulb lights up in spooky
situations

SNAKE PILLS

Charm those
snakes right out
of the trees!

Classic
Infrared Camera
'The Ghost-hunter's
invisible helper'

THINGS TO BUY
One X2W339.
I have had 100% success with this
machine in the past.
Three jars of EctoGel.
Very effective stuff.
Six X2W445s.
Set them up around the house.
Anyone crossing the invisible beam
will be caught on film. Perfect for
catching fake ghosts in the night!

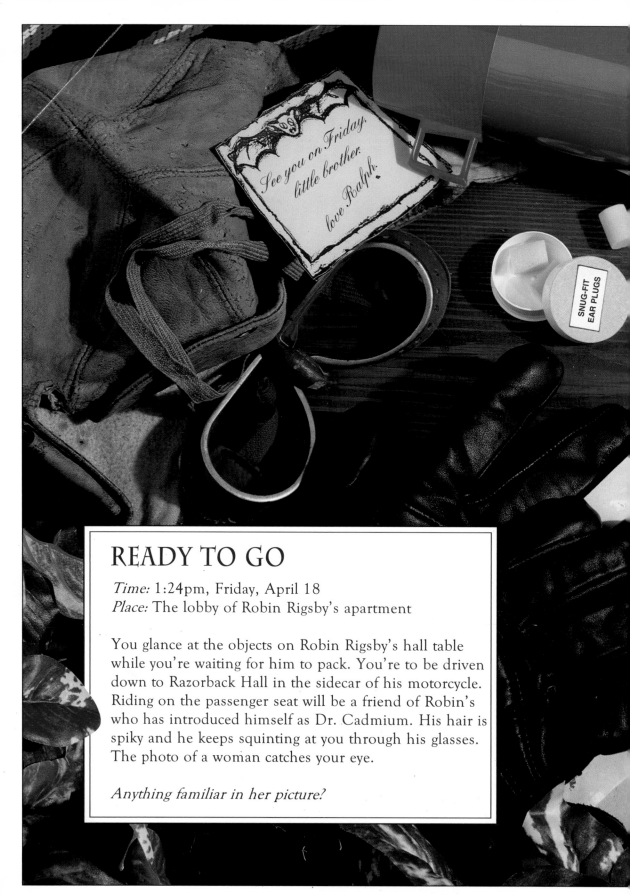

See you on Friday, little brother. love Ralph.

SNUG-FIT EAR PLUGS

READY TO GO

Time: 1:24pm, Friday, April 18
Place: The lobby of Robin Rigsby's apartment

You glance at the objects on Robin Rigsby's hall table while you're waiting for him to pack. You're to be driven down to Razorback Hall in the sidecar of his motorcycle. Riding on the passenger seat will be a friend of Robin's who has introduced himself as Dr. Cadmium. His hair is spiky and he keeps squinting at you through his glasses. The photo of a woman catches your eye.

Anything familiar in her picture?

Geo Collywobbles
Travel-Sick
Pills

GAMBLER'S GAZETTE

MONTHLY

You are cordially inv

A WEEKEND PA
at Razorback Ha

April 18th – April

Dear Robin,

So you're really going to do it! I
wonder if you'll have the nerve.
Here's that photo of me you asked for.

Yours forever,

Mercedes

Rigsby
m Street

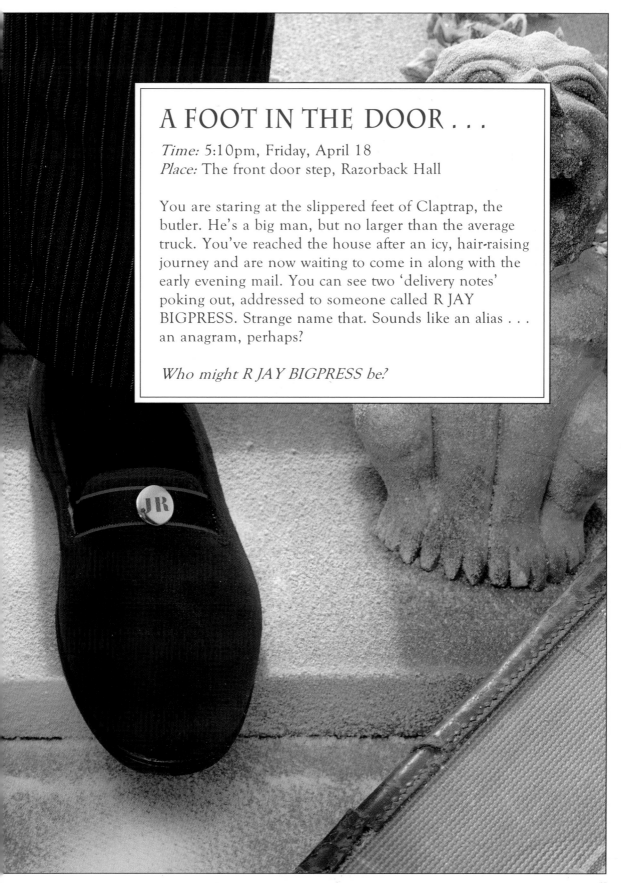

A FOOT IN THE DOOR . . .

Time: 5:10pm, Friday, April 18
Place: The front door step, Razorback Hall

You are staring at the slippered feet of Claptrap, the butler. He's a big man, but no larger than the average truck. You've reached the house after an icy, hair-raising journey and are now waiting to come in along with the early evening mail. You can see two 'delivery notes' poking out, addressed to someone called R JAY BIGPRESS. Strange name that. Sounds like an alias . . . an anagram, perhaps?

Who might R JAY BIGPRESS be?

Uncle Frank

Aunt Matilda

The two brothers

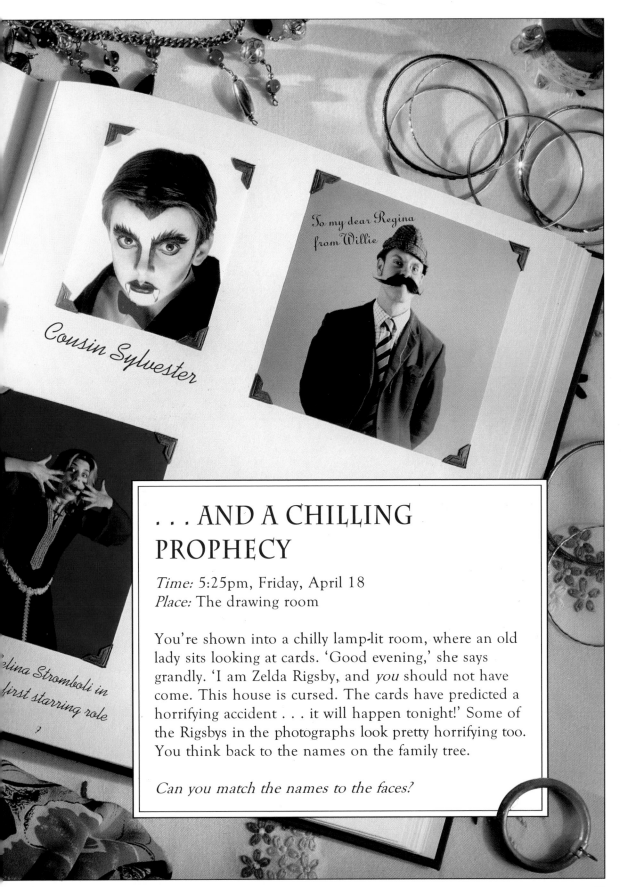

To my dear Regina from Willie

Cousin Sylvester

Zelina Stromboli in first starring role

. . . AND A CHILLING PROPHECY

Time: 5:25pm, Friday, April 18
Place: The drawing room

You're shown into a chilly lamp-lit room, where an old lady sits looking at cards. 'Good evening,' she says grandly. 'I am Zelda Rigsby, and *you* should not have come. This house is cursed. The cards have predicted a horrifying accident . . . it will happen tonight!' Some of the Rigsbys in the photographs look pretty horrifying too. You think back to the names on the family tree.

Can you match the names to the faces?

DINNER IS SERVED

Time: 8:22pm, Friday, April 18
Place: The Dining Room, with the family assembled

Colonel Bloodheart has arrived in his vintage car, and you've all sat down to eat. The Colonel is on your right. He's the one with the rough hands and table manners to match. The food is strange too. Maybe that's why Robin has left the table. You're glad you brought the house plans with you. They take your mind off the meal.

Where's your bedroom on the plan?

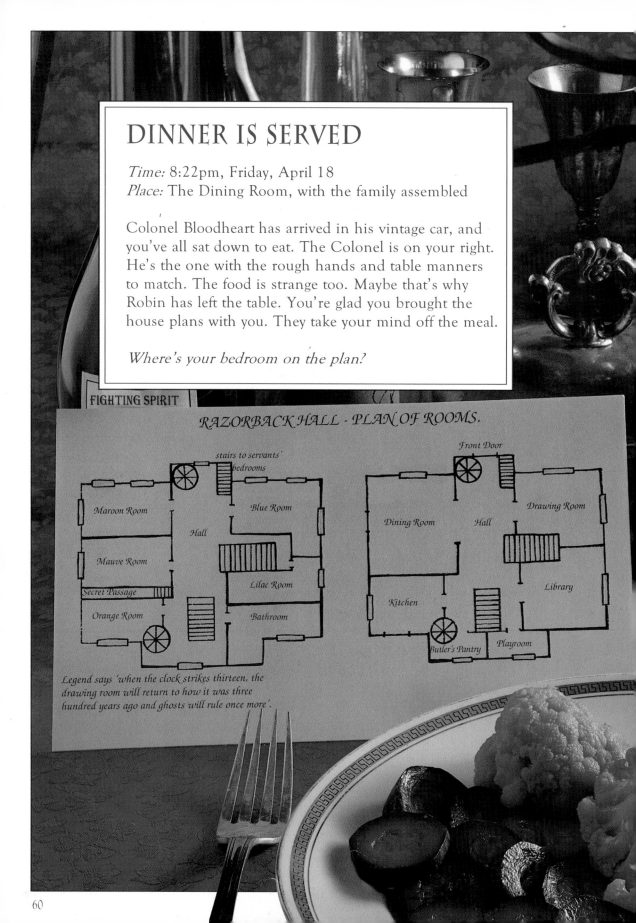

FIGHTING SPIRIT

RAZORBACK HALL - PLAN OF ROOMS.

stairs to servants' bedrooms

Maroon Room

Blue Room

Hall

Mauve Room

Lilac Room

Secret Passage

Orange Room

Bathroom

Front Door

Dining Room

Hall

Drawing Room

Kitchen

Library

Butler's Pantry

Playroom

Legend says 'when the clock strikes thirteen, the drawing room will return to how it was three hundred years ago and ghosts will rule once more'.

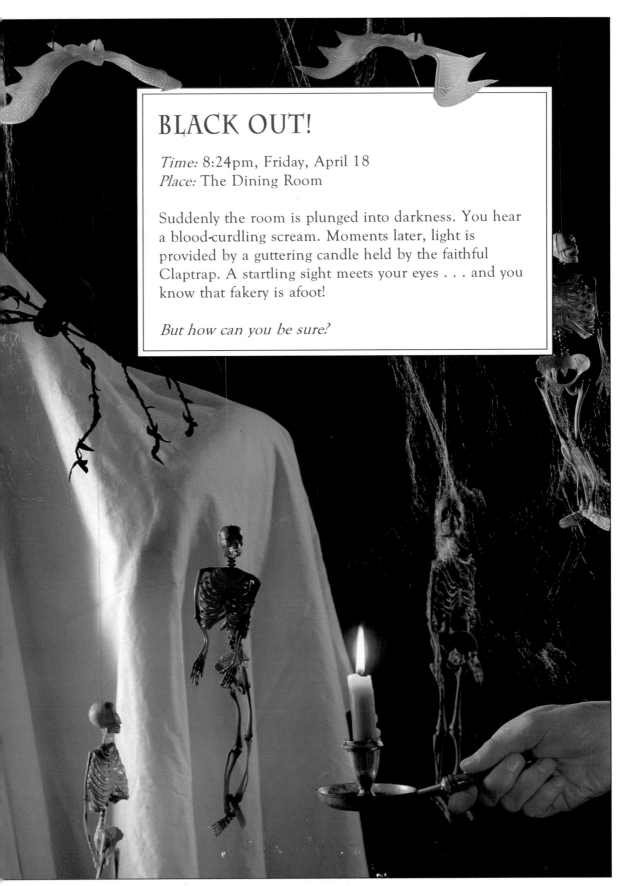

BLACK OUT!

Time: 8:24pm, Friday, April 18
Place: The Dining Room

Suddenly the room is plunged into darkness. You hear
a blood-curdling scream. Moments later, light is
provided by a guttering candle held by the faithful
Claptrap. A startling sight meets your eyes . . . and you
know that fakery is afoot!

But how can you be sure?

SABOTAGE!

Time: 8:31 pm, Friday, April 18
Place: The Generator Room, filled with junk

You've followed the butler into the darkness. He's turned the generator back 'ON', and the power has returned. But was it a *human* hand that turned it off in the first place? You've smeared some *EctoGel* on items in this graveyard for old machinery. It's time to test for any supernatural presences.

What are the results of the EctoGel *test?*

THE FIEND AT THE WINDOW

Time: 1:02am, Saturday, April 19
Place: In bed, after setting up the infrared cameras
in the hall

Outside a storm is raging and you can't sleep. Suddenly
you see a terrifying figure pressed up against the
window, lit up by a tremendous flash of lightning. But,
as you stare in horror, an eerie scratching sound comes
from behind the book-lined wall to your left. You leap
out of bed to investigate the noise – leaving that creepy
monster safely locked out.

What lies behind that wall?

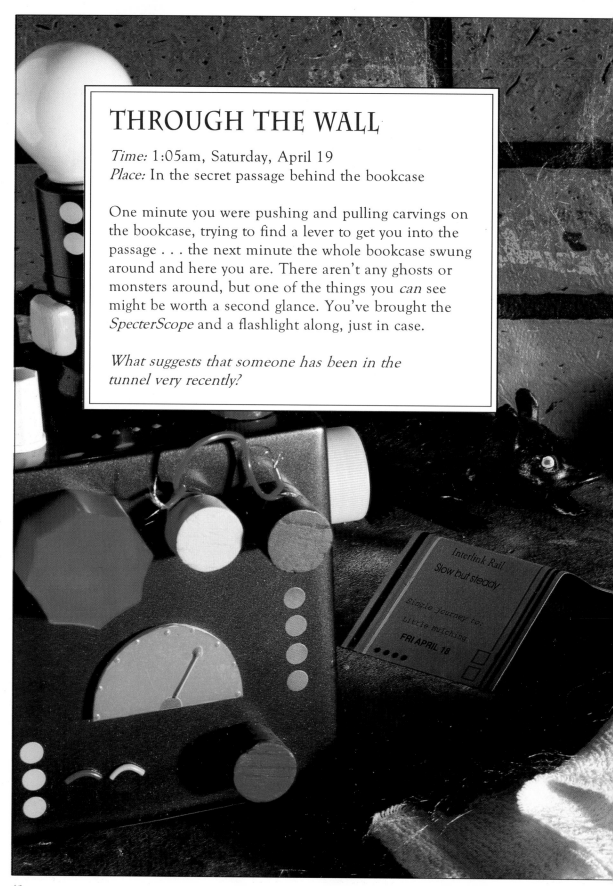

THROUGH THE WALL

Time: 1:05am, Saturday, April 19
Place: In the secret passage behind the bookcase

One minute you were pushing and pulling carvings on
the bookcase, trying to find a lever to get you into the
passage . . . the next minute the whole bookcase swung
around and here you are. There aren't any ghosts or
monsters around, but one of the things you *can* see
might be worth a second glance. You've brought the
SpecterScope and a flashlight along, just in case.

*What suggests that someone has been in the
tunnel very recently?*

Interlink Rail
Slow but steady

Single journey to:
Little Mulching
FRI APRIL 18

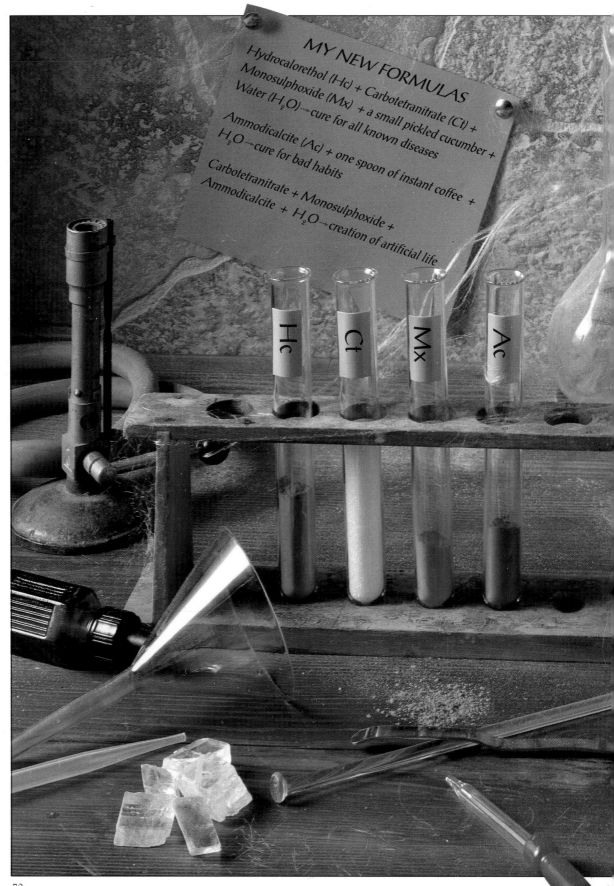

MY NEW FORMULAS

Hydrocalorethol (Hc) + Carbotetranitrate (Ct) +
Monosulphoxide (Mx) + a small pickled cucumber +
Water (H_2O)→cure for all known diseases

Ammodicalcite (Ac) + one spoon of instant coffee +
H_2O→cure for bad habits

Carbotetranitrate + Monosulphoxide +
Ammodicalcite + H_2O→creation of artificial life

INTO THE DEPTHS

Time: 1:34am, Saturday, April 19
Place: In the cellar

The secret passage has led you here, where – to your utter amazement – you find Dr. Cadmium has set up a laboratory. He's busy mixing powdered chemicals from three dishes with water in a flask marked 'X'. 'I've been experimenting down here all night,' he claims. 'This formula I'm mixing is my life's work . . . it is my life!' He laughs strangely.

Which formula is the doctor following?

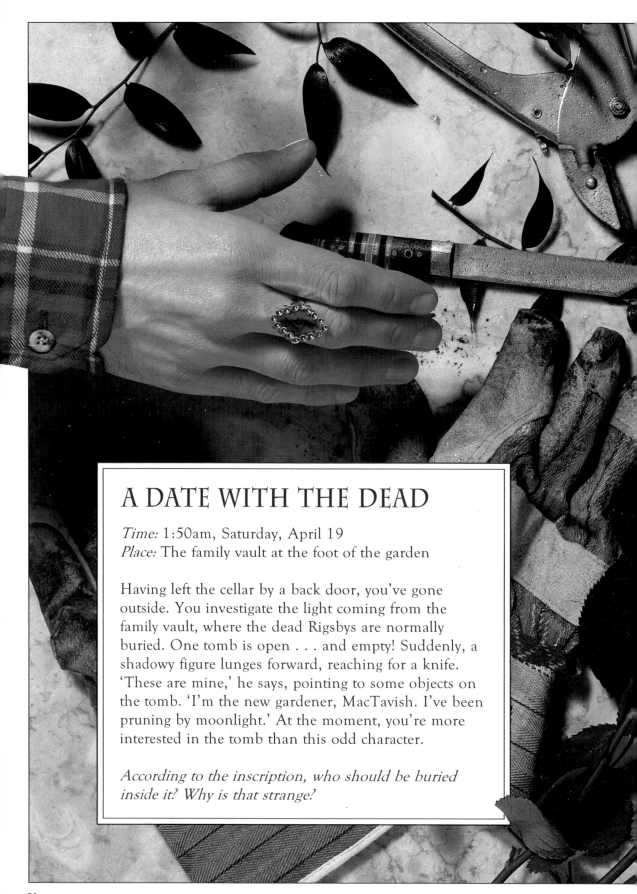

A DATE WITH THE DEAD

Time: 1:50am, Saturday, April 19
Place: The family vault at the foot of the garden

Having left the cellar by a back door, you've gone outside. You investigate the light coming from the family vault, where the dead Rigsbys are normally buried. One tomb is open . . . and empty! Suddenly, a shadowy figure lunges forward, reaching for a knife. 'These are mine,' he says, pointing to some objects on the tomb. 'I'm the new gardener, MacTavish. I've been pruning by moonlight.' At the moment, you're more interested in the tomb than this odd character.

According to the inscription, who should be buried inside it? Why is that strange?

THIS MAN WAS SON OF EBENEEZER
AND LIVED HIS LIFE WITH MERIT
BUT SADLY NEVER OWNED THE HOUSE
SINCE YOUNGER SONS DON'T INHERIT

IT'S ALIVE!

Time: 1:50am, Saturday, April 19
Place: The family vault at the foot of the garden

Heading back to the House of Horror, your eye is
caught by a human hand, sticking up among the flowers
. . . *with twitching fingers.* After investigation, you
discover to your amazement that the arm isn't real.
Bending closer to see what makes the fingers move, you
try to decipher the puzzling message lying in the soil.

What does it say?

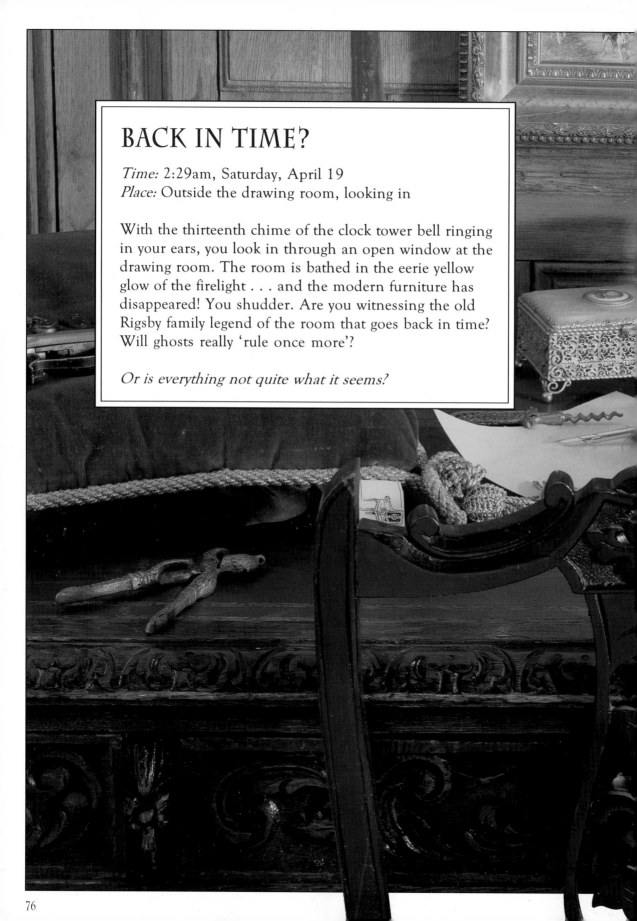

BACK IN TIME?

Time: 2:29am, Saturday, April 19
Place: Outside the drawing room, looking in

With the thirteenth chime of the clock tower bell ringing in your ears, you look in through an open window at the drawing room. The room is bathed in the eerie yellow glow of the firelight . . . and the modern furniture has disappeared! You shudder. Are you witnessing the old Rigsby family legend of the room that goes back in time? Will ghosts really 'rule once more'?

Or is everything not quite what it seems?

THE COLONEL TRIPS UP

Time: 2:38am, Saturday, April 19
Place: In the hall, at the foot of the stairs

Passing through the hall, on your way to your bedroom, you almost stumble over a body on the floor. It's Colonel Bloodheart . . . but his groans tell you there's life in him yet! 'This house should be mine,' he mutters. You can see what has caused his 'accident' — a length of green wire stretched across the floor. When he tripped across it, the statuette fell from its heavy pedestal, narrowly missing the colonel's head.

Have you seen that wire before?

SALE NOW ON
...244 5369

Memorial Marrow Missing

...scandal has hit ...ped the old time ...mmunity of Little ...hing as it was ...ed that this ...er of the...

Little Mulching Gazette Friday April 18

...mium Claims to Hold ...ey to Eternal Life

...life may become more than just a dream within ...xt few years, claims eminent genetic scientist Dr. ...topher Cadmium.

...My life's work is nearly complete,' the doctor told ...udience at the Golden Lightbulb Bright Ideas awards ...emony last week . 'I have succeeded in creating an ...ificial human who lives and breathes like you and I. ...on the world will know my genius, and I shall be able ...afford a new lab coat.'

Dr. Cadmium receiving a trophy at the Golden Lightbulb Bright Ideas awards ceremony

Spooky mansion good for business

The famous ghouls and ghosts of Razorback Hall have attracted many celebrities over the centuries, but none as famous as Arthur T. Bunkum, the oil millionaire, businessman and celebrity tiddlywink player. Now Mr. Bunkum has decided to go into the haunted house business himself. 'I am interested in buying Razorback Hall and turning it into a tourist attraction,' said the tycoon yesterday. Asked what price he is offering for Razorback Hall, he said: 'I won't discuss that. Let us just say that for the right house I would certainly go up to $20 million. But Razorback Hall has to be *proven* to be haunted. I'm not investing in no fake haunted house.'

Mr Bunkum is 65.

Kid-glove Burglar Still at Large

The escaped convict ...own as the Kid-glove ...ar is still roaming free ...ittle Mulching area. ...has now kept the ...abitants of the town in ...rip of fear for over four ...ks.

...utenant Pigeon of the ...Mulching police said ...This evil must stop. ...nformation about ...gloves'

Opposition

There are however many who oppose Dr. Cadmium's work. 'This man is evil,' says one leading critic. 'He is creating a Frankenstein's monster.' Dr. Cadmium is aware of the criticism. 'It is true that my human prototype has not been an unqualified success. He's a bit scary looking, and liable to outbursts of unpredictable violence. Still, it's just a teething problem. And, just to be on the safe side I carry my secret formula with me wherever I go.' Dr. Cadmium is a close friend of Robin Rigsby, brother of Sir Ralph, the new owner of Razorback Hall.

Stanislaus Distil **Science Correspondent**

Ghosts in the family

The recent spate of claimed hauntings at Razorback Hall, known as 'The House of Horror', is nothing new to the Rigsby family, *writes Gillian Blitz*. The Rigsbys have owned the spirit-infested mansion fo over 400 years. In that tim no less than 73 de members of the Rigsby o have been sighted in house and the grounds, s with their heads - other

One of the most fam all the Rigsby family is Billy Rigsby, w drowned by a cook i vat of soup in th kitchens in 1732 says that Billy ne the kitchens as a – a noisy, mischi who throws o creates havoc.

On othe

Cook's corn Sheep lu - Dog given More abc Prize M Cow

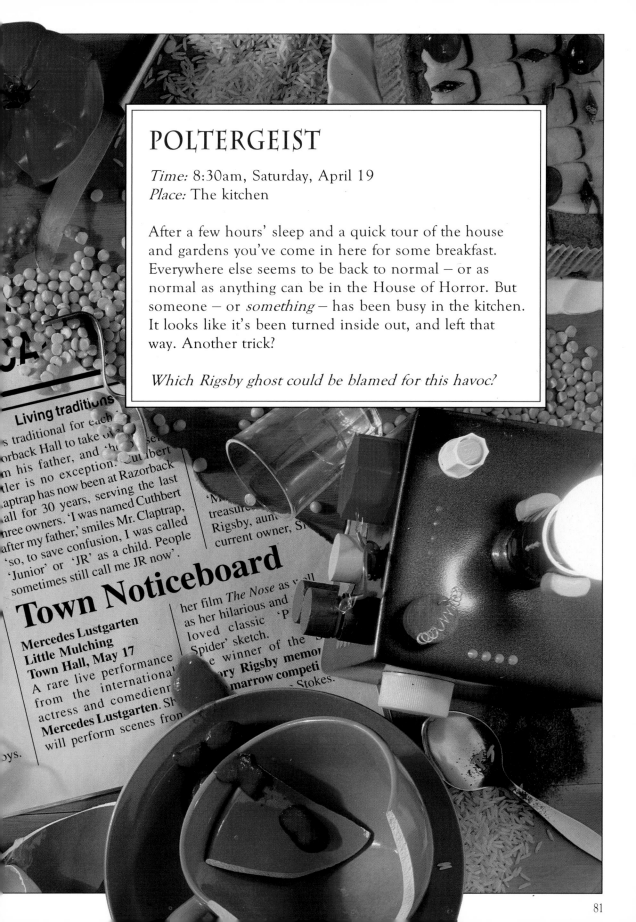

POLTERGEIST

Time: 8:30am, Saturday, April 19
Place: The kitchen

After a few hours' sleep and a quick tour of the house and gardens you've come in here for some breakfast. Everywhere else seems to be back to normal – or as normal as anything can be in the House of Horror. But someone – or *something* – has been busy in the kitchen. It looks like it's been turned inside out, and left that way. Another trick?

Which Rigsby ghost could be blamed for this havoc?

Living traditions

s traditional for each
orback Hall to take ... ser
m his father, and 'he...
tler is no exception. Cuthbert
aptrap has now been at Razorback
all for 30 years, serving the last
hree owners. 'I was named Cuthbert
after my father,' smiles Mr. Claptrap,
'so, to save confusion, I was called
'Junior' or 'JR' as a child. People
sometimes still call me JR now'.

'M...
treasure...
Rigsby, aun...
current owner, S...

Town Noticeboard

Mercedes Lustgarten
Little Mulching
Town Hall, May 17
A rare live performance
from the internationa...
actress and comedienr...
Mercedes Lustgarten. Sh...
will perform scenes fro...

her film *The Nose* as ... ll
as her hilarious and ...
loved classic 'P...
Spider' sketch.
e winner of the ...
ry Rigsby memor...
marrow competi...
Stokes.

oys.

INTERESTING DEVELOPMENTS

Time: 8:30am, Saturday, April 19
Place: In Dr. Cadmium's cellar laboratory – an ideal
photographic darkroom

Time to develop the photos from the cameras you set up
in the hallway. Each picture was taken when someone
went through one of the invisible infrared beams in the
night. Removing the photos of yourself and the colonel,
you're left with a ridiculous selection of hand-shadow
puppets! The phone rings – it's Montgomery Fang.
'How's it all going?' he asks. 'I'd love to be there, but
I've still got bat pox.' You're hardly listening. Something
is missing from the laboratory since last night . . .

What is it?

Me and Stuffing on holiday

Rigsby on Top of the World

Robin Rigsby can't get enough adventure at home – so he's planning a Himalayan expedition. 'I'm trying to raise the money,' says Robin. 'My target is about $2 million.'

For Robin, whose family have owned famously haunted Razorback Hall for generations, exploring runs in the family. 'My uncle Ja was an explorer, and he nothing – except man crocodiles. And the no terrors for me. I' many creepy thi home to b

SOMETHING IN THE PANTRY

Time: 9:17am, Saturday, April 19
Place: The butler's pantry

While no one is around, it makes sense to have a
quick peek in Claptrap's den. He's got an interesting
scrapbook, full of newspaper clippings about the
Rigsby family. The article about Jasper Rigsby looks
particularly fascinating.

*Jasper Rigsby? JR? Where have you seen those
initials before?*

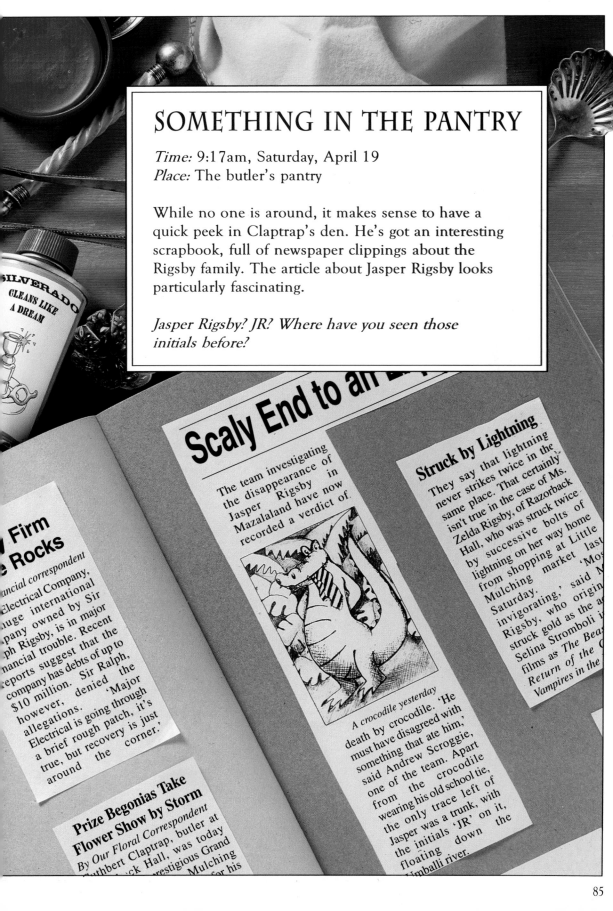

Scaly End to an E...

The team investigating
the disappearance of
Jasper Rigsby in
Mazalaland have now
recorded a verdict of

A crocodile yesterday

death by crocodile. 'He
must have disagreed with
something that ate him,'
said Andrew Scroggie,
one of the team. Apart
from the crocodile
wearing his old school tie,
the only trace left of
Jasper was a trunk, with
the initials 'JR' on it,
floating down the
...mballi river.

Struck by Lightning

They say that lightning
never strikes twice in the
same place. That certainly
isn't true in the case of Ms.
Zelda Rigsby, of Razorback
Hall, who was struck twice
by successive bolts of
lightning on her way home
from shopping at Little
Mulching market last
Saturday. 'Mos...
invigorating,' said N...
Rigsby, who origin...
struck gold as the a...
Selina Stromboli i...
films as *The Bea...
Return of the C...
Vampires in the ...

**...y Firm
...e Rocks**

...ancial correspondent
...Electrical Company,
...uge international
...pany owned by Sir
...ph Rigsby, is in major
...nancial trouble. Recent
...eports suggest that the
company has debts of up to
$10 million. Sir Ralph,
however, denied the
allegations. 'Major
Electrical is going through
a brief rough patch, it's
true, but recovery is just
around the corner.'

**Prize Begonias Take
Flower Show by Storm**

By Our Floral Correspondent
...uthbert Claptrap, butler at
...ck Hall, was today
...restigious Grand
... Mulching
... for his

85

THROUGH THE KEYHOLE

Time: 11:03am, Saturday, April 19
Place: Outside the playroom,
        looking in through the keyhole

Passing through the hall, you've heard voices. Peeping through the keyhole in the playroom door, you see the edge of someone's blue and white apron and hear snatches of a conversation. 'You know, Cuthbert, I hope Sir Ralph is scared off. I could turn this place into a nice home for retired housekeepers if it wasn't for them Rigsbys.' You hurry away before you're caught spying.

Who is talking to whom?

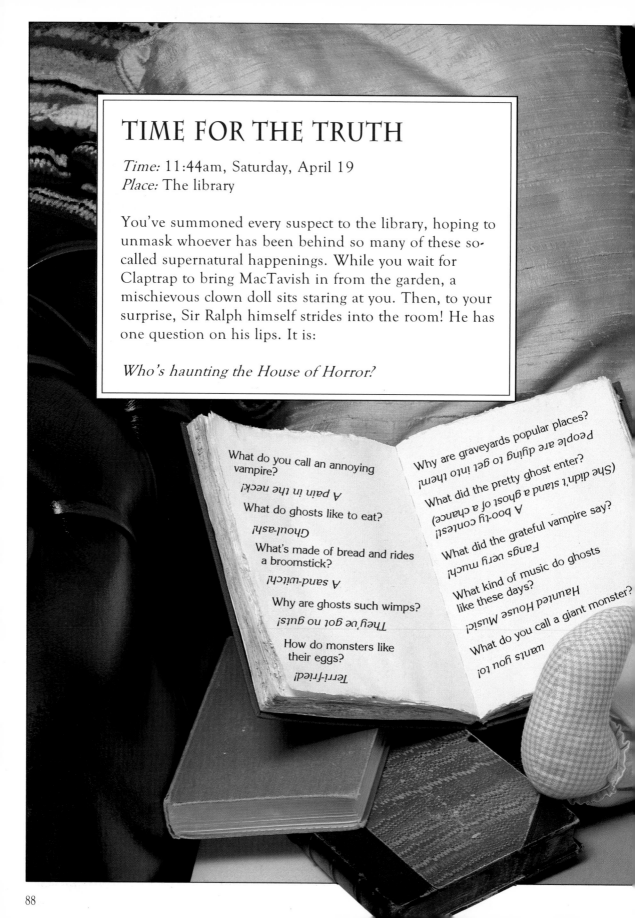

TIME FOR THE TRUTH

Time: 11:44am, Saturday, April 19
Place: The library

You've summoned every suspect to the library, hoping to unmask whoever has been behind so many of these so-called supernatural happenings. While you wait for Claptrap to bring MacTavish in from the garden, a mischievous clown doll sits staring at you. Then, to your surprise, Sir Ralph himself strides into the room! He has one question on his lips. It is:

Who's haunting the House of Horror?

What do you call an annoying vampire?

A pain in the neck!

What do ghosts like to eat?

Ghoul-ash!

What's made of bread and rides a broomstick?

A sand-witch!

Why are ghosts such wimps?

They've got no guts!

How do monsters like their eggs?

Terri-fried!

Why are graveyards popular places?

People are dying to get into them!

What did the pretty ghost enter?

A boo-ty contest! (She didn't stand a ghost of a chance)

What did the grateful vampire say?

Fangs very much!

What kind of music do ghosts like these days?

Haunted House Music!

What do you call a giant monster?

Whatever it wants you to!

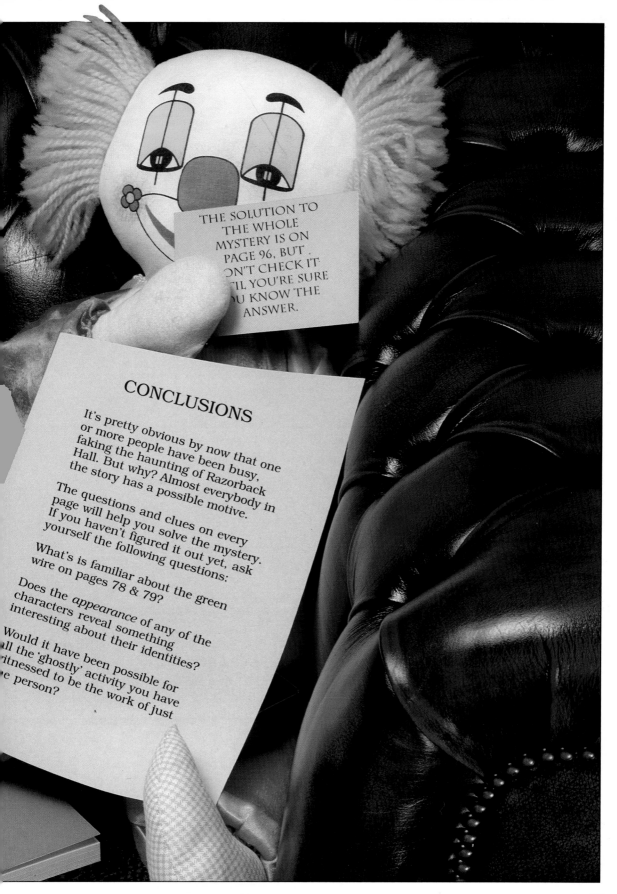

THE SOLUTION TO
THE WHOLE
MYSTERY IS ON
PAGE 96, BUT
DON'T CHECK IT
UNTIL YOU'RE SURE
YOU KNOW THE
ANSWER.

CONCLUSIONS

It's pretty obvious by now that one or more people have been busy, faking the haunting of Razorback Hall. But why? Almost everybody in the story has a possible motive.

The questions and clues on every page will help you solve the mystery. If you haven't figured it out yet, ask yourself the following questions:

What's is familiar about the green wire on pages 78 & 79?

Does the *appearance* of any of the characters reveal something interesting about their identities?

Would it have been possible for all the 'ghostly' activity you have witnessed to be the work of just one person?

HELPFUL HINTS

PAGES 50 & 51
The answers to both questions lie in the family tree.

PAGES 52 & 53
Match Fang's spooky shopping list to the objects in front of you.

PAGES 54 & 55
The clue's in her clothes.

PAGES 56 & 57
Can the letters can be shuffled to form a name you've seen before? On page 50 perhaps?

PAGES 58 & 59
Think about names and name *changes*.

PAGES 60 & 61
Fang gave you the name of your room — and mentioned something else about it too.

PAGES 62 & 63
Will any of your new ghostbusting equipment help you here?

PAGES 64 & 65
The *EctoGel* is green. What does green mean?

PAGES 66 & 67
The plan of the house should come in handy.

PAGES 68 & 69
A date could be part of an important clue.

PAGES 70 & 71
Start by matching the three powdered chemicals in the dishes with those in the test tubes. Then study the formulas.

PAGES 72 & 73
The answers are in the family tree again.

PAGES 74 & 75
Try taking away some of those 'E's.

PAGES 76 & 77
Does anything label this as a set-up?

PAGES 78 & 79
You've seen a ball of green wire among someone's possessions.

PAGES 80 & 81
Find the newspaper story about a poltergeist.

PAGES 82 & 83
'X' used to mark the spot.

PAGES 84 & 85
At the 'foot' of pages 56 and 57 perhaps?

PAGES 86 & 87
Who'd want to set up a home for retired housekeepers? Where have you seen the name Cuthbert before?

PAGES 88 & 89
Have you found the answer to *every* question? If not, go through the story again before reaching your conclusion . . .

ANSWERS

PAGES 50 & 51

The notes below the tree tell you that Razorback Hall always belongs to the *eldest male blood relative* in the Rigsby family. Apart from Ralph, all the members of the Rigsby family on the tree are ruled out either because they're deceased (dead), female, non-blood relations or not the eldest. Therefore Ralph must be the rightful owner of the house.

The only other possible claimant is Jasper Rigsby. He is presumed dead by the family, but his body was never found.

If you look at the family tree on Professor Fang's desk, you'll see that Ralph's younger brother is called Robin. This must be the 'Master Robin' mentioned by Fang.

PAGES 52 & 53

You need to identify the unnamed items on Fang's shopping list. If you look at the cards by the objects on the shelves, you'll see that X2W339 is the *SpecterScope*. X2W445 is on a card by the infrared camera top left, so this must be the camera

Fang wants you to buy six of. According to his shopping list, they are *'perfect for catching fake ghosts in the night'*.

PAGES 54 & 55

The distinctive green and orange scarf worn by Mercedes Lustgarten in the photograph on page 55 is the same one worn by the mysterious woman on page 52. It could well have been Mercedes in the Paranormal Emporium.

PAGES 56 & 57

The name R JAY BIGPRESS can be rearranged to make JASPER RIGSBY. We know from page 50 that this is the name of Ralph and Robin's uncle, supposedly eaten by a crocodile in Mazalaland. So who's using his name now, in such a mysterious way? And why?

PAGES 58 & 59

Uncle Frank, Aunt Matilda and Cousin Sylvester are named under their pictures. Everyone else can be identified from what you have learned about them on the family tree on page 50.

One of the figures in the photo of '*the two brothers*' is Sir Ralph Rigsby. Therefore the other must be Robin, his brother.

The man with the moustache has inscribed his picture '*To my dear Regina from Willie*'. Regina Rigsby's husband is called Colonel W. Bloodheart. The 'W' could stand for 'Willie', so this is probably the Colonel in the photo.

We know that Zelda Rigsby's movie name was Selina Stromboli. Therefore the final picture, of '*Selina Stromboli in her first starring role*', must be the young Zelda.

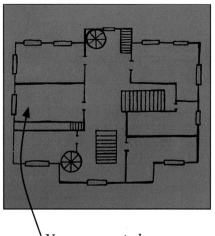

Your room is here.

PAGES 60 & 61

In Professor Fang's '**_AN IMPORTANT WARNING TO THE READER_**' on page 49, he tells you that he's arranged for 'you to sleep in the Mauve room'. He also says that it was 'once said to be the most haunted room in the whole house.'

PAGES 62 & 63

One of your new gadgets, the *SpecterScope*, is clearly visible in the bottom left corner of page 62. On page 53, in the Paranormal Emporium, you read that the *SpecterScope* '*lights up in spooky situations*'. However, in

the candle-lit dining room, the bulb on the machine is still firmly off. This helps to confirm that all these ghostly goings-on are fake.

PAGES 64 & 65

EctoGel '*turns purple in the presence of the Paranormal*', according to the card in the shop on page 53. However, the *EctoGel* spread around in the Generator Room is still *green*. This indicates that nothing supernatural has happened there.

PAGES 66 & 67

Look at the plan of the house again. In one wall of the Mauve Room is a window onto the garden – this is the one that the monster is peering through. But behind the book-lined wall to your left . . . is a secret passage! This must be where the sound is coming from.

PAGES 68 & 69

The 'Interlink Rail' train ticket lying in the shadows has the date '**FRI APRIL 18**' on it. That's yesterday's date. That means that whoever dropped it has been in the passage since then.

But this raises another mystery. You, Robin and Dr. Cadmium came by motorcycle. Colonel Bloodheart came in his vintage car. Claptrap, Mrs. Stuffing and Zelda were already in the house. So who arrived by *train*?

PAGES 70 & 71

The purple mixture in the glass flask marked '**X**' is probably made up of the powdered red, white and blue chemicals beside it. The very same three chemicals are also contained in three of the test tubes in the rack on the left. They have the shortened names 'Ct', 'Mx' and 'Ac'.

If you now look at Dr. Cadmium's list of 'NEW FORMULAS', you'll see that the full names for these three chemicals are Carbotetranitrate, Monosulphoxide and Ammodicalcite. And, according to Dr. Cadmium, together with water they make a formula for the creation of artificial life!

PAGES 72 & 73

The inscription on the tomb describes the deceased as the '**SON OF EBENEEZER**'. If you refer back to the Rigsby family tree on page 50, you will see that Ebeneezer Rigsby only had two sons: Digory and Jasper. The inscription goes on to say that this tomb belongs to the '**YOUNGER SON**'. That could only mean Jasper.

But we know from page 50 that Jasper Rigsby disappeared on an expedition in Mazalaland, assumed eaten alive by a crocodile. So this tomb cannot possibly have contained the body of Jasper Rigsby, alive or dead.

PAGES 74 & 75
This note was encoded by adding the letter 'E' between every other letter. If you take away all the extra 'E's, you are left with:

This arm's up and running ready for our visitor to find. Destroy this once you've read it.

This note was clearly not intended for your eyes. It sounds more like an exchange between *accomplices*.

PAGES 76 & 77
If you look closely you will notice that the cushion on the left of the desk has a label attached to it. The label has a little picture of an antique chair on it — the same picture that appears on 'DEADWOOD & SONS' delivery note on page 56. Their business is renting antique furnishings. This is no time-slip. The old furniture has been hired!

PAGES 78 & 79
There's only one place where you've seen any green wire like that before. That's on Robin Rigsby's hall table, in among his travel items.

PAGES 80 & 81
The newspaper story on page 80, entitled '**Ghosts in the Family**', mentions the ghost of Billy Rigsby, who was said to haunt the kitchen. He's supposed to be a poltergeist - a spirit who likes to make a mess. If he exists, this is just the sort of mess he might make!

PAGES 82 & 83

All the items from the night before are present and correct . . . except the beaker containing formula 'X'.

PAGES 84 & 85

The initials JR have turned up twice before in the story. First, as the monogrammed initials on Claptrap's slippers on pages 56 & 57. Second, in the newspaper story, '**Ghosts in the Family**' on page 80, where Claptrap says: 'I was called 'Junior' or 'JR' as a child. People sometimes still call me JR now.' No connection with Jasper Rigsby there then.

PAGES 86 & 87

The speaker must be Mrs. Stuffing, the housekeeper. Who else would want the Rigsbys away from the house so she could set up a home for retired housekeepers?

Her invisible companion is none other than Claptrap the butler. We know his first name is Cuthbert from the newspaper article '**Ghosts in the Family**' on page 80.

PAGES 88 & 89

There are a lot of creepy things and double-dealings going on at the House of Horror. But there is only one true explanation for the 'haunting'.

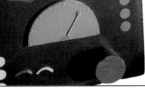

You must use your detective powers of reasoning. Try to find the answers to all the questions and carefully examine all the visual clues. Then, when you are *sure* you know who's haunting the House of Horror, turn to page 96 and hold the solution up to a mirror . . .

SOLUTION

There's one thing in common with most of the 'supernatural' things you've seen at Razorback Hall. They are fakes. But who is responsible, and why? An important clue lies in the newspaper article about Arthur T. Bunkum, on page 80. He's a millionaire who's very anxious to buy a creepy old mansion, but, as he says: 'it has to be proven to be haunted. I'm not investing in no fake haunted house.'

One of the newspaper clippings in Claptrap's scrapbook on pages 84 & 85 reveals that Sir Ralph Rigsby has got BIG money problems — he needs ten million dollars immediately to save his company, the Major Electrical Co. If Sir Ralph could sell Razorback Hall to Arthur T. Bunkum, then his money problems would be over.

In the photographs of Sir Ralph on Professor Fang's desk on pages 50 & 51, and with his brother Robin on page 58, Ralph is shown wearing an unusual ring with a red stone. The same ring appears on the hand of MacTavish, the strange 'new gardener', you met by the tomb on pages 72 & 73. One of the keys on MacTavish's key ring matches one in Claptrap's pantry tagged 'Generator Room'. This was the key Sir Ralph, disguised as MacTavish, used to get into the generator room to switch the power off during dinner on pages 60 & 61. Sir Ralph had come down, in disguise, by train — dropping his ticket in the secret passage on page 68.

Ralph needed someone to confirm that the house really was haunted again . . . that's where you fitted in. If he could trick you into believing that the hauntings were genuine, then Arthur T. Bunkum might buy the house. No wonder Sir Ralph was so eager to plant the idea that his uncle, Jasper Rigsby, had come back from the dead by faking an open tomb on pages 72 & 73 — don't forget the delivery note from Jack Mason ('marble carving a speciality') on page 56.

But that's not the whole story. He must have had help. When he was in the secret passage, someone had to be at the window on pages 66 & 67. The note left beside the mechanical arm was from one schemer to another. Then there was all that rented antique furniture. Ralph couldn't have moved it all into place without the help of . . . his brother, Robin. He was the one who had left the dining table just before the power was switched off. He was the one controlling the dinner-time 'ghosts'.

Think back to that green wire stretched across the hall floor, which tripped Colonel Bloodheart up. It came from the ball of wire on Robin's lobby table on page 55. Robin needed money too, to fund his trip to the Himalayas. If Arthur T. Bunkum bought Razorback Hall, both brothers would get what they want. Ralph and Robin haunted the 'House of Horror'.

But they needn't have bothered. The bulb on the SpectreScope is lit up for the first and only time in the kitchen on pages 80 and 81, which means that there was genuine paranormal activity at work in the room. Billy Rigsby, the family poltergeist, is back in action . . . perhaps Arthur T. Bunkum will buy the house after all!

PORT...

AN IMPORTANT MESSAGE TO T... READER FROM KING ALVIN

Dear Reader and most loyal friend,

As one of my closest and most trusted knights, I am sending you on a mission of the greatest importance. All is not well at Portcullis Castle. Reports have reached me that the lord of the castle, Baron Toadfettle, has turned against me and has hatched an evil plot.

According to my sources, the Baron has either taken, or is about to take, one of my knights prisoner. I have no idea which one it might be, as my knights are fighting in all four corners of the Earth.

You must enter Portcullis Castle through a secret passage and make contact with the magician Haggard. Though trusted by Baron Toadfettle he is a loyal friend of mine. Together, you must find out WHO'S THE PRISONER OF PORTCULLIS CASTLE.

Do not fail me, brave knight. The wars abroad do not go well, and I must keep peace here in my own land. I am relying on you.

King Alvin.

This story was
written by
**Phil Roxbee Cox
& Rupert Heath**

photographed by
Sue Atkinson
and designed by
Joe Pedley.

The series editor was
Gaby Waters.

With thanks to
John Russell
& Jo Litchfield

On every double page, there are questions that need to be answered. These are there to keep you thinking and to help you find out just what's going on at the castle. When you've reached page 137, you should be able to say who the prisoner is. If you get stuck, there are hints on page 138, answers on pages 139 to 143, and the solution is on page 144.

Spell 133

FOR ESCAPING FROM ANYWHERE

To escape from anywhere
 you will need:
A bird's feather
A drop of red candle wax
A rusty nail
A Vandusian snail

Place them all in a row,
Shout out where you want to go . . .
And you'll be free!

Spell 1

BEARD

To leng
 follov
A bearde
Some str
Four horses
Much luck

Attach the ho
beard with the
clockwise thre
saying: 'Fol-d
today this bear
LONGER!' Then
galloping as fa

STAR
SOCIETY
for Magicians,
Wizards, Warlocks
itches.

Musical potion
for Lady Olivia
(This should
improve
her frightful
lute-playing.)

Haggard
Magician
People-into-Toads
a Speciality

has been elect...
THE STAR SO...
for Magicians, Sor...
Warlocks

...l visit to the futu...
More camera film
Baseball cap
More pon...

The Magician's Lair

Time: Monday, a little before three o'clock
Place: Haggard's room in Portcullis Castle

The secret passage has brought you out here, into a
room packed with every kind of magical potion you can
imagine, and crawling with snails and toads. Suddenly,
there's a puff of green smoke. It's Haggard, the king's
friend and secret enemy of the evil Baron Toadfettle.
There's powerful magic at work here!

Where does Haggard get his magical powers from?

...eness potion
for Baroness
Toadfettle
(Olivia's mother).
An elixir to help
the old dragon
smile more
easily.

...need my Magic Gem if
My spells are to succeed.
Its sparkle is the source
Of all the power I need.
If it's lost, my magic's gone
And I'll grow weak indeed.

Mirth
Mixture

A potion for
Chester, Baron T.'s
awful jester. This
should make him fizz!

Remember:
Sir Clifford, the B...on's
food taster, ...ful
poison antidote
...dangero...

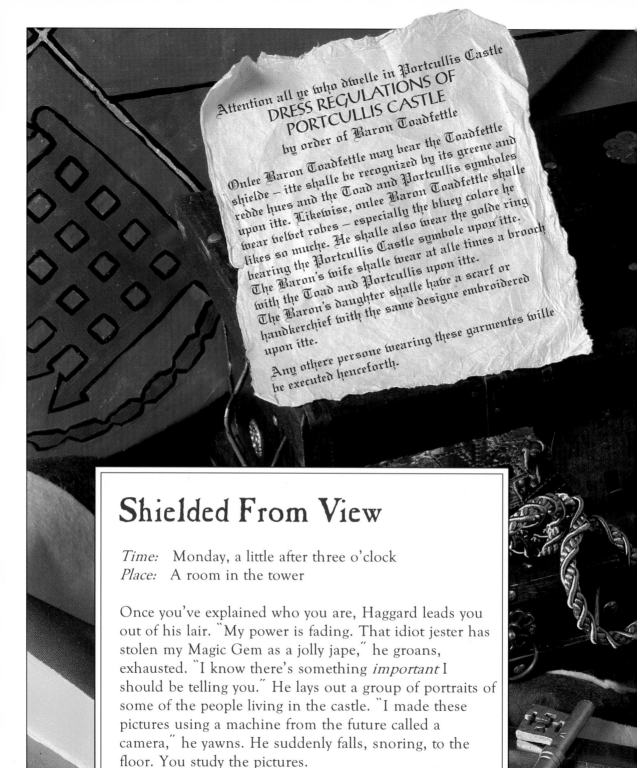

Attention all ye who dwelle in Portcullis Castle

DRESS REGULATIONS OF
PORTCULLIS CASTLE

by order of Baron Toadfettle

Onlee Baron Toadfettle may bear the Toadfettle shielde – itte shalle be recognized by its greene and redde hues and the Toad and Portcullis symboles upon itte. Likewise, onlee Baron Toadfettle shalle wear velvet robes – especially the bluey colore he likes so muche. He shalle also wear the golde ring bearing the Portcullis Castle symbole upon itte.

The Baron's wife shalle wear at alle times a brooch with the Toad and Portcullis upon itte.

The Baron's daughter shalle have a scarf or handkerchief with the same designe embroidered upon itte.

Any othere persone wearing these garmentes wille be executed henceforth.

Shielded From View

Time: Monday, a little after three o'clock
Place: A room in the tower

Once you've explained who you are, Haggard leads you out of his lair. "My power is fading. That idiot jester has stolen my Magic Gem as a jolly jape," he groans, exhausted. "I know there's something *important* I should be telling you." He lays out a group of portraits of some of the people living in the castle. "I made these pictures using a machine from the future called a camera," he yawns. He suddenly falls, snoring, to the floor. You study the pictures.

Can you put a name to every face?

The Baron's food taster

The Baron's jester

Food For Thought

Time: Monday, just gone four o'clock
Place: The castle kitchen

Leaving the power-drained magician in a deep sleep,
you disguise yourself as a servant and slink into the
kitchens. This is probably as good a place as any to
pick up Castle gossip. You carry some carrots over to
an enormous table and begin to peel them. "I've lost
my ring!" screams a man in a high-pitched voice. You
recognize the Baron's food taster, Sir Clifford. "It must
have come off when I was inspecting the food. A gold
piece for anyone who finds it!"

Can you find the missing ring?

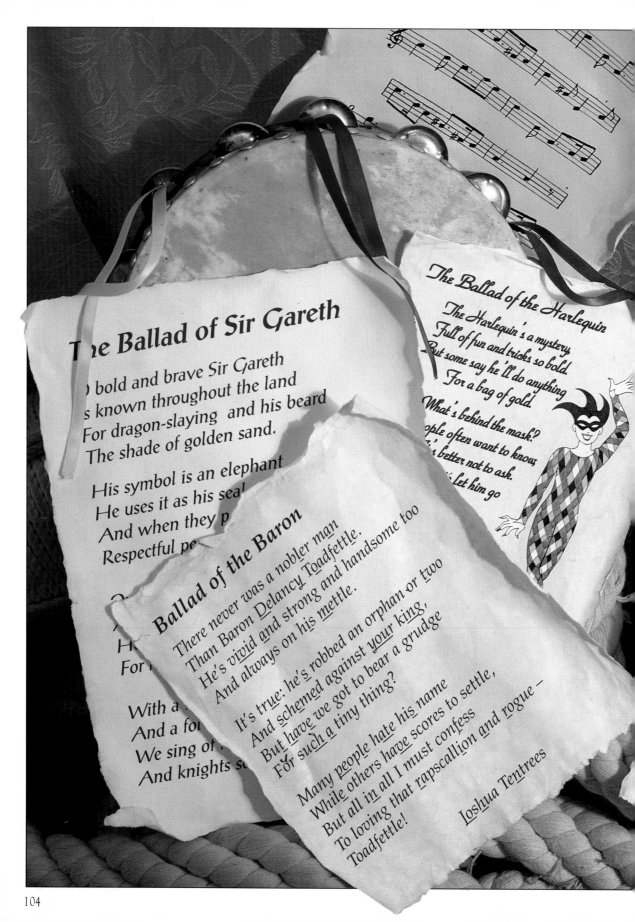

The Ballad of Sir Gareth

bold and brave Sir Gareth
known throughout the land
For dragon-slaying and his beard
The shade of golden sand.

His symbol is an elephant
He uses it as his sea'
And when they p
Respectful pe

With a
And a fo
We sing of
And knights s

Ballad of the Baron

There never was a nobler man
Than Baron Delancy Toadfettle.
He's vivid and strong and handsome too
And always on his mettle.

It's true: he's robbed an orphan or two
And schemed against your king,
But have we got to bear a grudge
For such a tiny thing?

Many people hate his name
While others have scores to settle,
But all in all I must confess
To loving that rapscallion and rogue –
Toadfettle!

Joshua Tentrees

The Ballad of the Harlequin

The Harlequin's a mystery,
Full of fun and tricks so bold.
But some say he'll do anything
For a bag of gold.

What's behind the mask?
ople often want to know,
's better not to ask.
's let him go

Music, Music, Music!

Time: Monday, sometime after six o'clock
Place: The minstrels' gallery

No gold piece from Sir Clifford for finding his ring, just a clip around the ear! But he did mention that there's to be a special banquet later tonight in the castle's great hall. Still disguised as a servant, you take a quick look at the hall from up in the minstrels' gallery. There's no one around, but you spot a coded message.

What does it say?

In The Chapel

Time: Monday, at the stroke of seven
Place: The castle chapel

The coded message in the minstrels' gallery has led you
here. You're squeezed behind a cold stone pillar, out of
sight. The only other people in the chapel are a monk,
wearing a simple brown habit, and a girl in flowing
robes. From your hiding place, you can't see their faces.
"Were you followed, Lady Olivia?" asks the monk.
"No," replies the lady, her face still in shadow. He
hands her a sealed letter.

Who is the letter from?

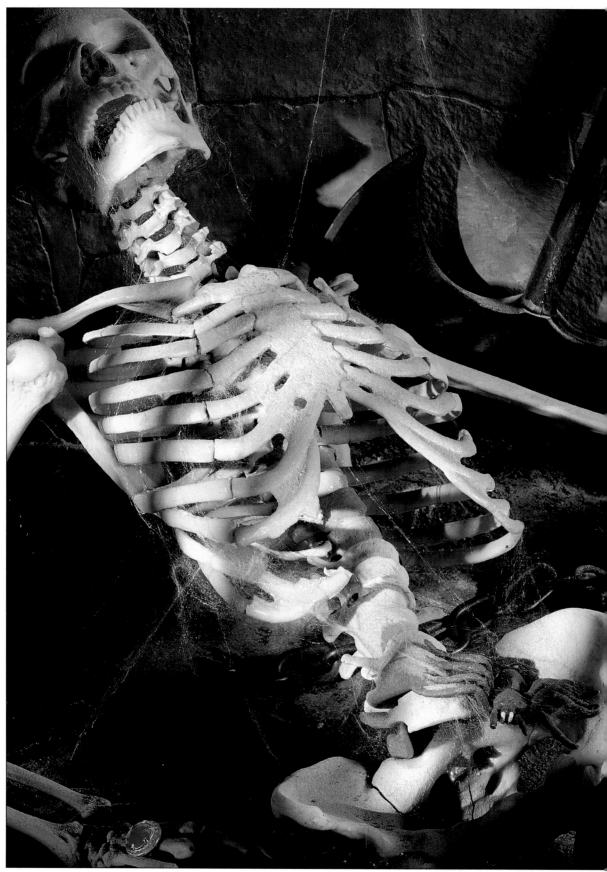

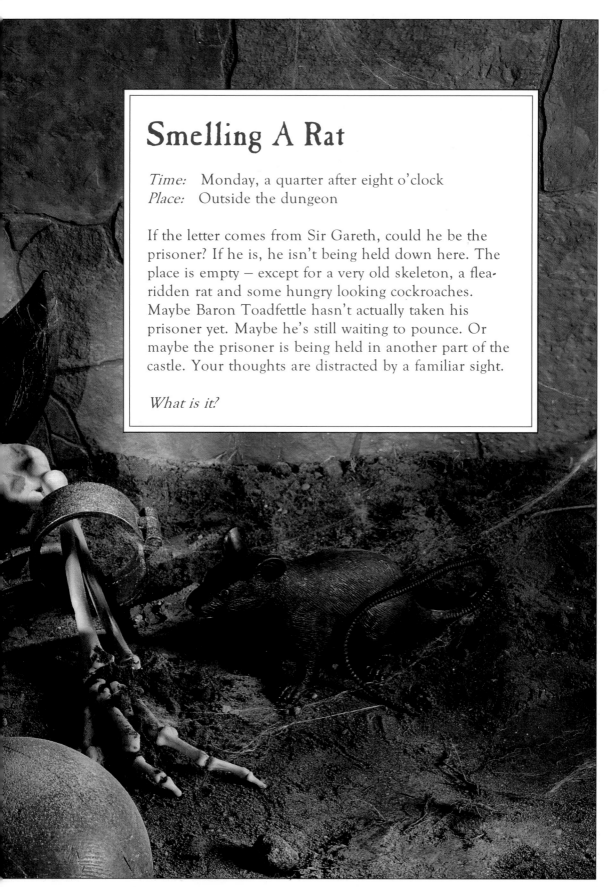

Smelling A Rat

Time: Monday, a quarter after eight o'clock
Place: Outside the dungeon

If the letter comes from Sir Gareth, could he be the
prisoner? If he is, he isn't being held down here. The
place is empty – except for a very old skeleton, a flea-
ridden rat and some hungry looking cockroaches.
Maybe Baron Toadfettle hasn't actually taken his
prisoner yet. Maybe he's still waiting to pounce. Or
maybe the prisoner is being held in another part of the
castle. Your thoughts are distracted by a familiar sight.

What is it?

Feasting Your Eyes

Time: Monday, eight o'clock
Place: The castle's great hall, during a banquet

You've hurried here from the dungeon. You don't want to miss any speeches Baron Toadfettle might make. Disguised as a squire this time, you help to serve the food. "A toast!" cries the Baron, getting to his feet. "To King Alvin . . . and to one of his closest friends, a *guest* in Portcullis Castle!" He laughs and throws himself back into his chair, grabbing a piece of meat. You spy a key on a gold chain around his neck.

Where have you seen a key like that already?

Possible Prisoners

1. Sir Gareth,
2. Sir Flaxen,
3. Sir Joan,

Sir Flaxen

Loyal knight to King
Nickname: Wandere
Main characteristic:
                    ve
                         bouts
                         fo

Sir Gareth

Loyal knight to King
Nickname: Goldenbea
Main characteristic:
disgustingly high level
of chivalry
Present whereabouts:
Unknown
History:
Son of Arthur
Leschampes of
Summerfield
Became an app
King Alvin at th
Ha   fought
seve foreign wars

of Jacob and Sarah
      Flaxen became King
           ever knight at the
      just ten years old. Since
            alongside the king on
            mpaigns, gathering
           t every opportunity.
            the battlefield
           f Katmandu, in
           mel lost their

My lord,

Please keep this missive safe for it
containeth secret information for your
eyes only.

The DRAGON is now ready to
be released — ready to spit fire and
strike fear into the hearts of all Baron
Toadfettle's enemies! Please come to its
secret chamber and witness for yourself
its lethal potential.

Long live Baron Toadfettle!
Down with King Alvin!

Sir Lee of Grimthorp
Master of the DRAGON

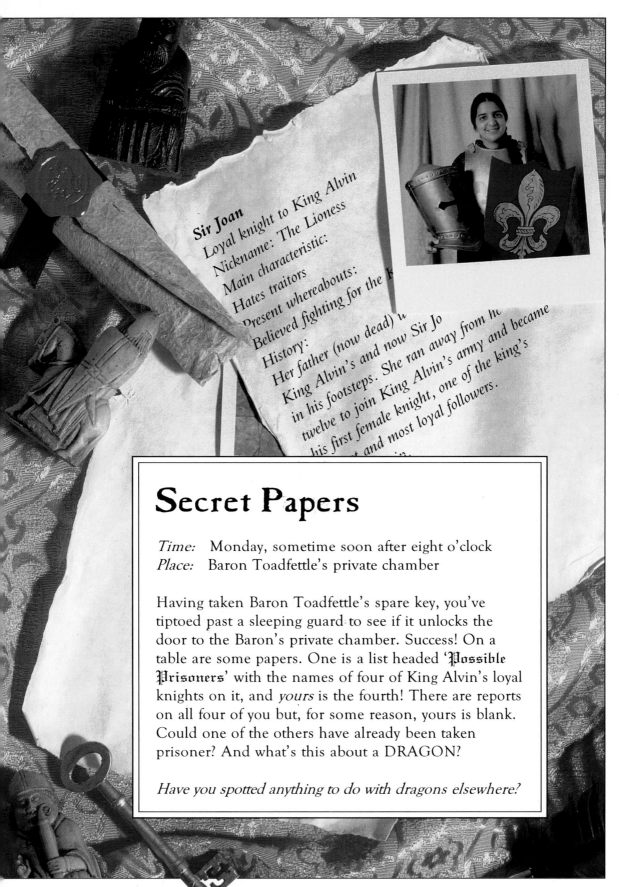

Sir Joan

Loyal knight to King Alvin

Nickname: The Lioness

Main characteristic:

Hates traitors

Present whereabouts:

Believed fighting for the K

History:

Her father (now dead) u

King Alvin's and now Sir Jo

in his footsteps. She ran away from h

twelve to join King Alvin's army and became

his first female knight, one of the king's

t and most loyal followers.

Secret Papers

Time:　Monday, sometime soon after eight o'clock
Place:　Baron Toadfettle's private chamber

Having taken Baron Toadfettle's spare key, you've tiptoed past a sleeping guard to see if it unlocks the door to the Baron's private chamber. Success! On a table are some papers. One is a list headed 'Possible Prisoners' with the names of four of King Alvin's loyal knights on it, and *yours* is the fourth! There are reports on all four of you but, for some reason, yours is blank. Could one of the others have already been taken prisoner? And what's this about a DRAGON?

Have you spotted anything to do with dragons elsewhere?

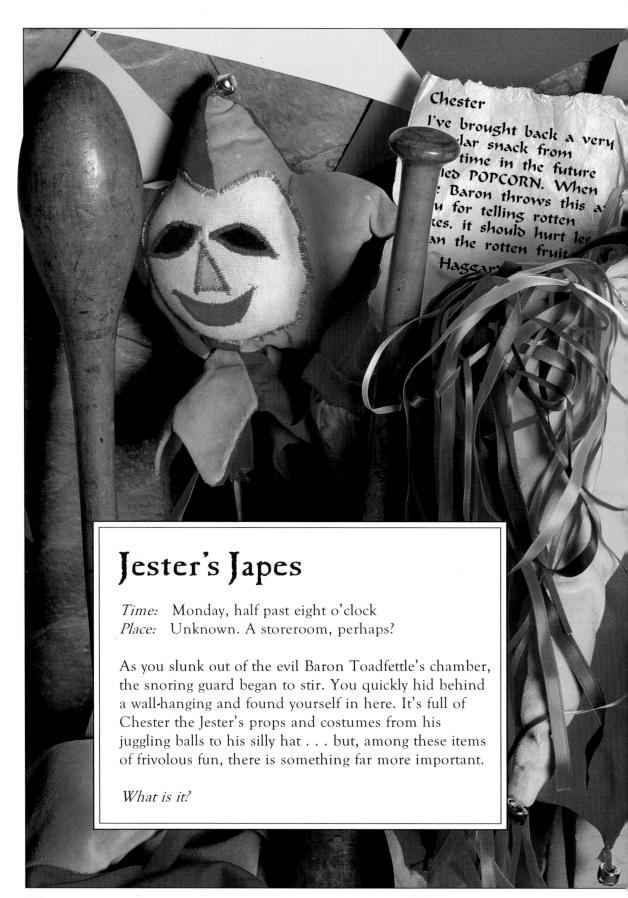

Chester
I've brought back a very
~~lar~~ snack from
~~a~~ time in the future
~~cal~~led POPCORN. When
~~the~~ Baron throws this a~~t~~
~~yo~~u for telling rotten
~~jok~~es, it should hurt les~~s~~
~~th~~an the rotten fruit~~.~~

Haggar~~t~~

Jester's Japes

Time: Monday, half past eight o'clock
Place: Unknown. A storeroom, perhaps?

As you slunk out of the evil Baron Toadfettle's chamber,
the snoring guard began to stir. You quickly hid behind
a wall-hanging and found yourself in here. It's full of
Chester the Jester's props and costumes from his
juggling balls to his silly hat . . . but, among these items
of frivolous fun, there is something far more important.

What is it?

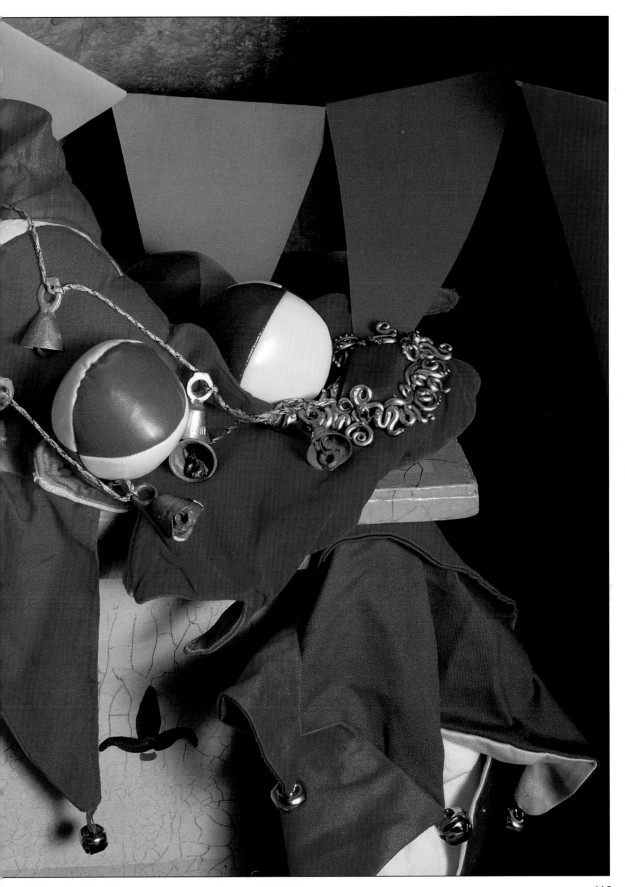

Let The Joust Begin

Time: Tuesday, early morning
Place: The jousting tent

You've given Haggard the Magic Gem but he still can't tell you who the prisoner of Portcullis Castle is. "I *know* there's something important I forgot to tell you," the wizard yawns, "but it'll take more than one night for my full powers to return."

He helps you to disguise yourself as a knight visiting the castle for the day's joust. "Keep the visor of your helmet down and call yourself the Green Knight," he says. "The evil Baron Toadfettle welcomes all jousting knights. No one will question why you're here." You are only half-listening. You've spotted a vital piece of information lurking among the weaponry.

What is it?

Sir Gawain's

Sir John's

The Baron's. HANDS OFF.

THE ORDER OF JOUST:
1. Sir John of Lockwood AGAINST
Robin, Comte de Jeune
2. Sir Joan AGAINST killed in battle
Sir Gawain de Aquitaine
3. 'The Black Knight' AGAINST
'The Green Knight'
4. 'The Glum Knight' AGAINST
'The Happy Knight'

The Game's Afoot

Time: Tuesday, midday
Place: Under Baron Toadfettle's chair at the joust

Ducking under a flap at the back of Baron Toadfettle's
tent, you find yourself face-to-heel with the Baron who
is seated on a raised platform. "King Alvin has a spy in
the castle," Sir Clifford whispers in his ear. "Just as you
predicted would happen. We found a secret passage
from the village that must have been used as the way
in." There's no doubt it's *you* they're talking about, but
you're distracted by a crumpled note on the ground.

Who is 'the Wanderer' mentioned in this note?

119

Long winter...
mail underwear, 1 pair...
Full metal jacket, 1
previous owner, very
good condition (a few
small arrow holes)
Contact
...rumblestone

REMINDER TO ALL PERSONNEL

The Room Without Locks, at
the top of the West Tower, has a
sprung door that is easy to open
from the outside but, once
opened, automatically swings
shut and stays shut. 'Tis not
possible to open it from within.
BE CAREFUL!

FOUND:
ONE
GAUNTLET
RETRIEVED
FROM A
VAT OF
BOILING OIL.

All contestants in the
...pcoming Tug-of-War
...with the soldiers of
...alliard Castle should
...t to the
...room for
...ard's special
...ening potio...

DIRECT ATTACK WAGON

No mention of the Direct
Attack Wagon may be made
by name. This highly secret
weapon, being made up of a
mighty bombard, or cannon,
mounted upon wheels and
disguised to appear like a
covered wagon or cart, must
only be referred to by the
agreed codename. Any
soldier failing in this d...
will be put to death.

By Order of BARON
TOADFETTLE

120

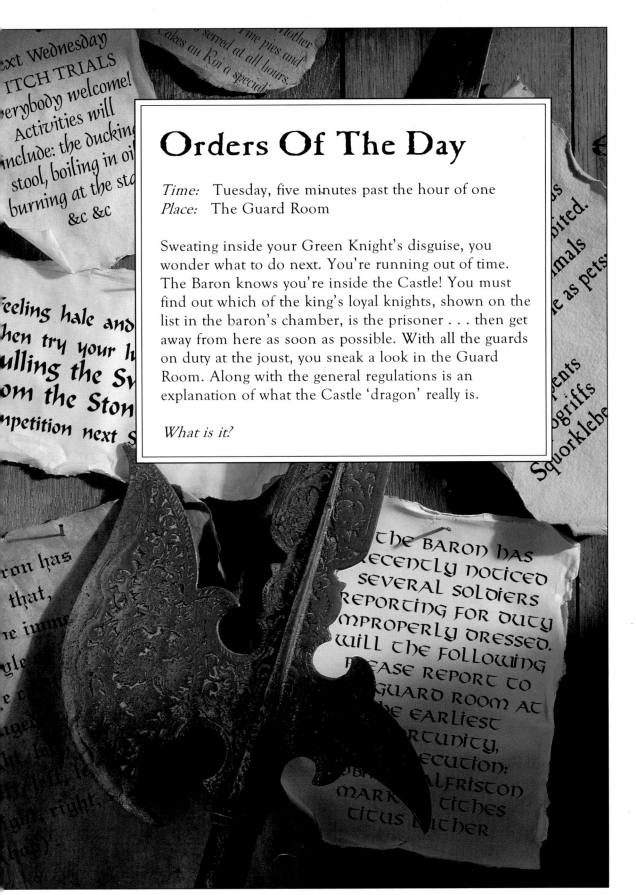

Orders Of The Day

Time: Tuesday, five minutes past the hour of one
Place: The Guard Room

Sweating inside your Green Knight's disguise, you wonder what to do next. You're running out of time. The Baron knows you're inside the Castle! You must find out which of the king's loyal knights, shown on the list in the baron's chamber, is the prisoner . . . then get away from here as soon as possible. With all the guards on duty at the joust, you sneak a look in the Guard Room. Along with the general regulations is an explanation of what the Castle 'dragon' really is.

What is it?

THE BARON HAS
RECENTLY NOTICED
SEVERAL SOLDIERS
REPORTING FOR DUTY
IMPROPERLY DRESSED.
WILL THE FOLLOWING
PLEASE REPORT TO
GUARD ROOM AT
THE EARLIEST
ORTUNITY,
ECUTION:
ALFRISTON
MARK TITHES
TITUS LITHER

My Lady's Chamber

Time: Tuesday, just before two o'clock
Place: Lady Olivia's chamber

With everyone at the joust, you search in here. Sir
Gareth is loyal to King Alvin and, if he's writing to
Olivia in secret, perhaps she can be trusted . . . but
first you need to know what was in his letter to her.
The Baron may be evil and an enemy of the king, but
that doesn't mean to say that his daughter has to be.

Where is the letter she was handed in the chapel?

My one love, my joy, my life,
I am still months away
from Portcullis Castle, fighting
? king in a far-off land.
? long to be close to
?nore! How sad I
?oyalty to King
?us from sharing our
?nly!
?Until we meet again, my
lily-white dove, my peach!

Your loving Gareth

Hidden Letters

Time: Tuesday, two o'clock
Place: Lady Olivia's chamber

You read Sir Gareth's letter to the Baron's daughter and
the odd reply that she has yet to send him. Sir Gareth's
letter is embarrassing though it makes it clear that he's a
long way from Portcullis Castle. But what if he comes
here? King Alvin did write that the Baron has 'either
taken, or is *about* to take, one of my knights prisoner'.
Then you spot a hidden message in Olivia's reply.

What does it say?

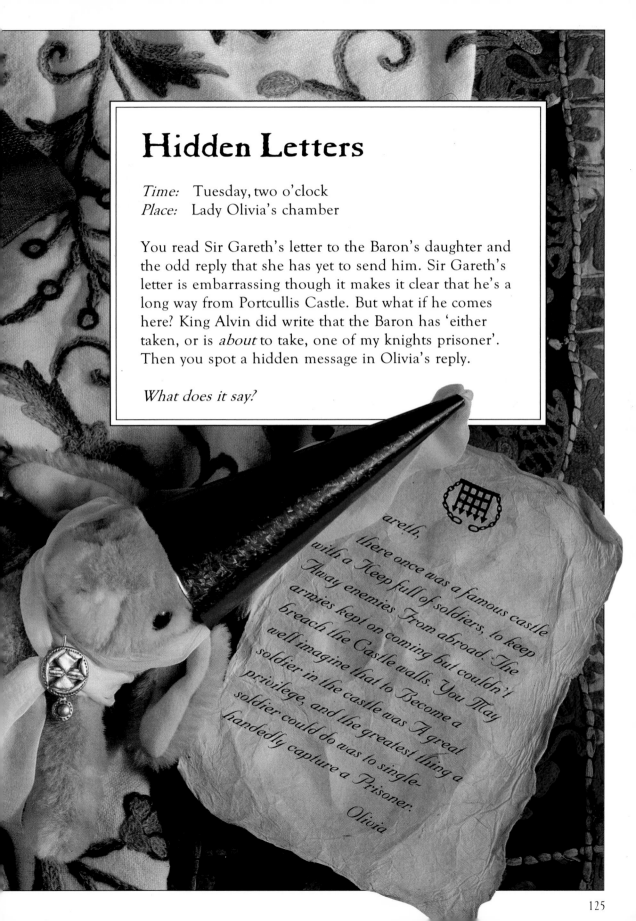

...areth,

there once was a famous castle
with a Keep full of soldiers, to keep
Away enemies From abroad. The
armies kept on coming but couldn't
breach the Castle walls. You May
well imagine that to Become a
soldier in the castle was A great
privilege, and the greatest thing a
soldier could do was to single-
handedly capture a Prisoner.

Olivia

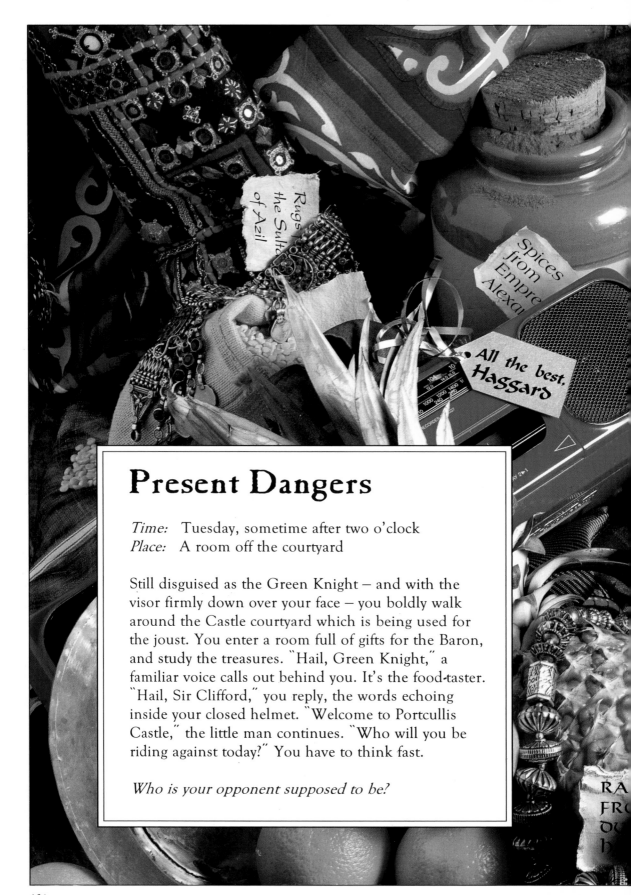

Present Dangers

Time: Tuesday, sometime after two o'clock
Place: A room off the courtyard

Still disguised as the Green Knight – and with the
visor firmly down over your face – you boldly walk
around the Castle courtyard which is being used for
the joust. You enter a room full of gifts for the Baron,
and study the treasures. "Hail, Green Knight," a
familiar voice calls out behind you. It's the food-taster.
"Hail, Sir Clifford," you reply, the words echoing
inside your closed helmet. "Welcome to Portcullis
Castle," the little man continues. "Who will you be
riding against today?" You have to think fast.

Who is your opponent supposed to be?

From Prince Henry

Exotic seeds

Magic Beans

Precious gems

Even more precious gems

Spices from the Orient

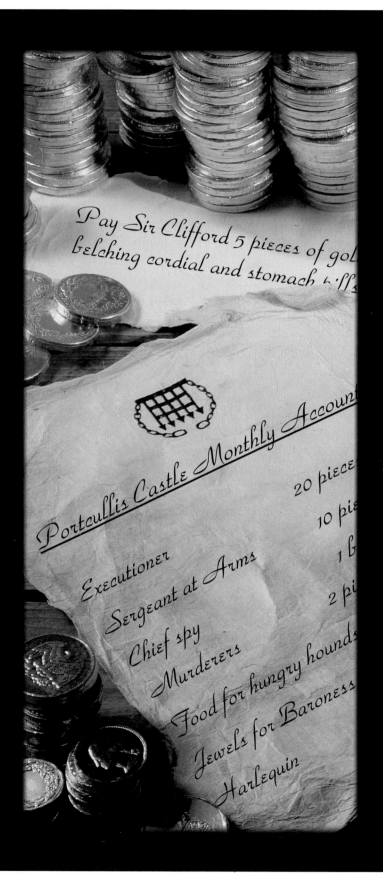

Pay Sir Clifford 5 pieces of gol
belching cordial and stomach pills

Portcullis Castle Monthly Account

Executioner   20 piece

Sergeant at Arms   10 pi

Chief spy   1 b

Murderers   2 pi

Food for hungry hounds

Jewels for Baroness

Harlequin

each
s of gold

NIL

1 bag of gold

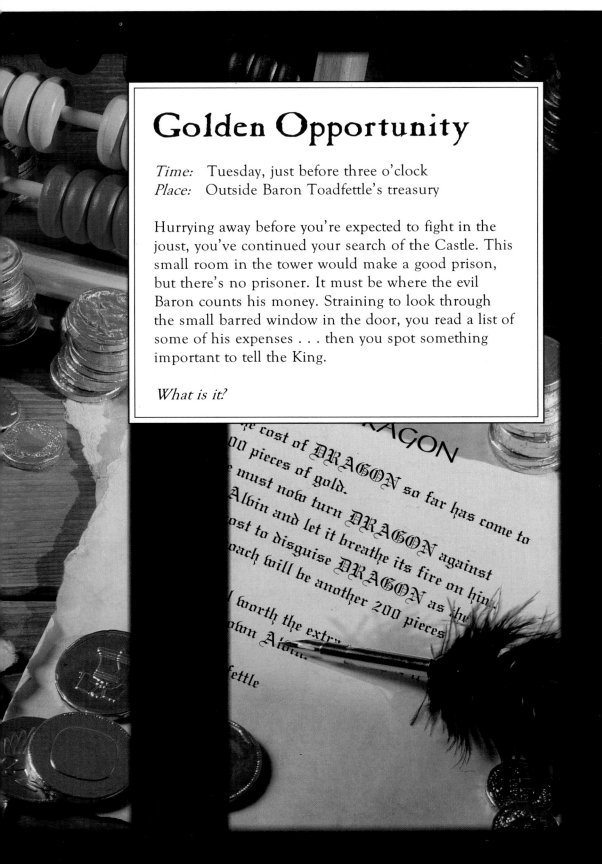

Golden Opportunity

Time: Tuesday, just before three o'clock
Place: Outside Baron Toadfettle's treasury

Hurrying away before you're expected to fight in the joust, you've continued your search of the Castle. This small room in the tower would make a good prison, but there's no prisoner. It must be where the evil Baron counts his money. Straining to look through the small barred window in the door, you read a list of some of his expenses . . . then you spot something important to tell the King.

What is it?

e cost of DRAGON so far has come to
00 pieces of gold.
e must now turn DRAGON against
Albin and let it breathe its fire on him.
ost to disguise DRAGON as the
oach will be another 200 pieces
l worth the extr
own Albin
fettle

A Dog's Life

Time: Tuesday, sometime after three o'clock
Place: The Castle kennels

You've read about hungry hounds in the castle accounts.
Perhaps one is guarding the prisoner? A trip to the
kennels might help. The building appears to be empty.
You lift your visor to take a closer look . . . and see
someone lying in the straw! Drawing your sword, you
step forward. "I know who you are," chuckles a voice
from the straw. "We can't talk here. Meet me on top of
the east tower at nightfall. Until then, let me sleep."

Who do you think the man in the straw is?

FANG

To The Battlements

Time: Tuesday, after dark
Place: The battlements of the east tower

Dressed as a squire, and wearing a fake bushy beard,
you're reading a note from the mysterious man in the
straw. It's attached to an arrow that just whistled past
your ear in the darkness — narrowly missing you — as
you waited for him to meet you on the ramparts as
promised. In the flickering candlelight you can see
that, for once, it's a message that isn't in code! If what
it says is true, the end to your quest is in sight.

But where is the Room Without Locks?

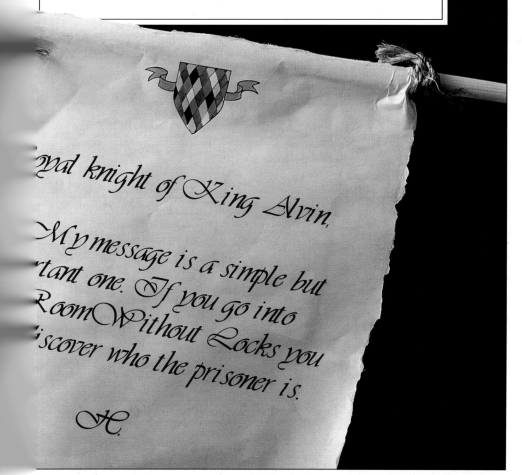

...yal knight of King Alvin,

My message is a simple but
...rtant one. If you go into
...Room Without Locks you
...iscover who the prisoner is.

H.

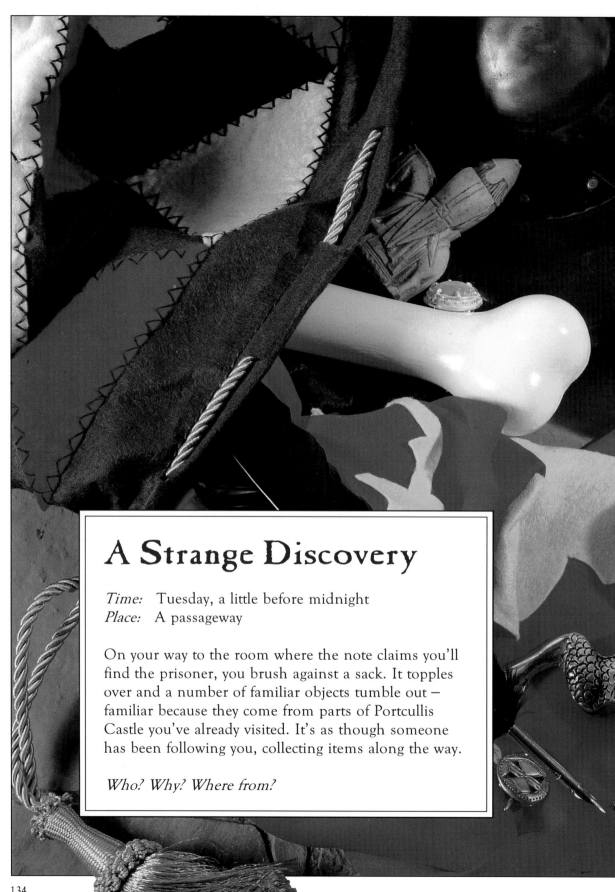

A Strange Discovery

Time: Tuesday, a little before midnight
Place: A passageway

On your way to the room where the note claims you'll find the prisoner, you brush against a sack. It topples over and a number of familiar objects tumble out – familiar because they come from parts of Portcullis Castle you've already visited. It's as though someone has been following you, collecting items along the way.

Who? Why? Where from?

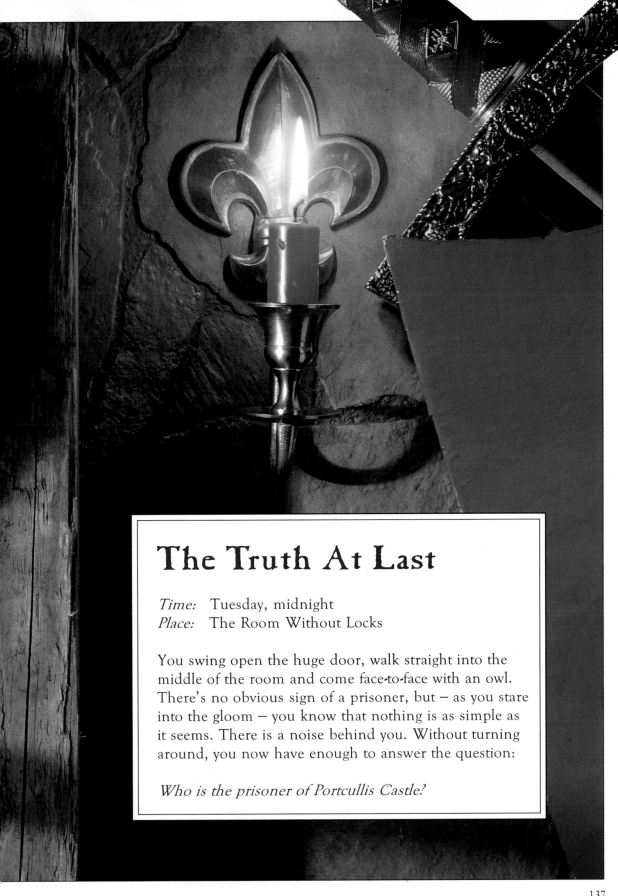

The Truth At Last

Time: Tuesday, midnight
Place: The Room Without Locks

You swing open the huge door, walk straight into the middle of the room and come face-to-face with an owl. There's no obvious sign of a prisoner, but – as you stare into the gloom – you know that nothing is as simple as it seems. There is a noise behind you. Without turning around, you now have enough to answer the question:

Who is the prisoner of Portcullis Castle?

The Helpful Hints

Pages 98 & 99
The reason's in a rhyme.

Pages 100 & 101
Any notions
from Haggard's
potions? The
dress regulations
should help you
with the rest.

Pages 102 & 103
Here's a golden
opportunity to use your eyes.

Pages 104 & 105
The answer is underlined.

Pages 106 & 107
An elephant might seal the
identity of the letter writer.

Pages 108 & 109
The skeleton will lend you a
hand in solving this puzzle.

Pages 110 & 111
Pages 100 & 101 will unlock
the mystery.

Pages 112 & 113
There's more than one kind
of dragon in this story . . .

Pages 114 & 115
What did Haggard say the
jester had stolen?

Pages 116 & 117
Your suspect list has
just shortened.

Pages 118 & 119
The Wanderer was last seen
on pages 112 & 113.

Pages 120 & 121
Could DRAGON be short
for something?

Pages 122 & 123
Look for the elephant again.

Pages 124 & 125
It stands out – in capitals!

Pages 126 & 127
The answer's in *black* and white
on pages 116 & 117.

Pages 128 & 129
What is the DRAGON to be
used for?

Pages 130 & 131
There's a clue at your fingertips –
and at his!

Pages 132 & 133
Go back to pages 120 & 121 for
a Reminder.

Pages 134 & 135
The bag tells you who and the
who tells you why.
Match every item in the picture
with locations you have
visited already.

Pages 136 & 137
You should know enough
about the Room Without
Locks to figure this out
on your own . . .

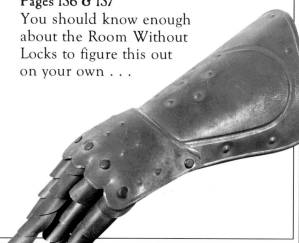

The Answers

Pages 98 & 99

Haggard gets all his magical powers from his Magic Gem. In a poem on page 99, Haggard says that the Magic Gem's **'sparkle is the source of all the power I need.'**

Pages 100 & 101

We know the names of the Baron's food taster and jester from papers on Haggard's table (page 99). The food taster is called Sir Clifford. The jester is called Chester.

The other three people can be recognized from the 'DRESS REGULATIONS OF PORTCULLIS CASTLE'. We know only the Baron is allowed to wear a blue velvet robe and a gold portcullis ring. Therefore the man standing in front of the Toadfettle shield must be Baron Toadfettle himself. The two women in the other picture can be identified in the same way. The Baron's wife, Baroness Toadfettle, is the one wearing the Toadfettle brooch and his daughter, Lady Olivia, is the one holding a handkerchief with the Toadfettle emblem on it.

Pages 102 & 103

The green and gold ring is hidden here.

Pages 104 & 105

The coded message is hidden in the **'Ballad of the Baron'** on page 104. To decode the message, read only the underlined letters. Once all the other letters have been removed, the message says:

LADY OLIVIA, I MUST SEE YOU IN THE CHAPEL AT SEVEN. FRIAR JOHN.

Pages 106 & 107

The letter bears a seal of an elephant. From the '*Ballad of Sir Gareth*' on page 104 we know that '*his symbol is an elephant, he uses it as his seal*'. Therefore this letter is most probably from him.

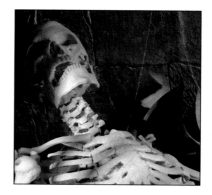

Pages 108 & 109

The skeleton is wearing a ring very similar to the one you found for Sir Clifford on pages 102 & 103! Actually this isn't the same one. Although it's the same design, it's much older and dirtier. Maybe this skeleton is one of Sir Clifford's ancestors – maybe he displeased one of the Baron's!

Pages 110 & 111

The key around Baron Toadfettle's neck is identical to the one lying on the table on page 100. It must be important.

Pages 112 & 113

You have come across three dragons so far in the story.

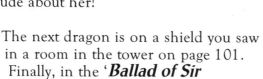

The first is mentioned on page 99 on a label on Haggard's table. He describes Baroness Toadfettle as an '*old dragon*' – but he's just being rude about her!

The next dragon is on a shield you saw in a room in the tower on page 101. Finally, in the '*Ballad of Sir Gareth*' (page 104), Sir Gareth is said to '*be known throughout the land for dragon-slaying*'.

Keep your eyes open for more dragons later.

Pages 114 & 115

Lying well-camouflaged on a piece of red cloth is . . . Haggard's Magic Gem!

You learned on page 100 that Chester the Jester had stolen the Magic Gem. Now that you've found it you can return it to Haggard and maybe restore his magical powers.

Pages 116 & 117

On the paper headed 'THE ORDER OF JOUST' it states that Sir Joan has been '*killed in battle*'. She was one of the four possible prisoners on pages 112 & 113. You can cross her off your list of possible prisoners now.

Pages 118 & 119

You've seen the name '*The Wanderer*' once before: on the paper about Sir Flaxen on page 112. 'The Wanderer' is his nickname. The note says that '*the Wanderer is still in foreign lands*'.

Pages 120 & 121

The notice on page 120 headed '**DIRECT ATTACK WAGON**' has certain letters bolder than the others. If these letters are taken alone they spell '**D-R-A-G-O-N**'. The so-called Dragon you keep hearing about is a shortened form of '**DIRECT ATTACK WAGON**' – a '**highly secret weapon**' which is 'disguised to appear like a covered wagon'.

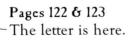

Pages 122 & 123

The letter is here.

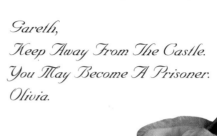

Pages 124 & 125

To decode the hidden message in Olivia's letter, read only the words beginning in a capital letter. The message then says:

Gareth,
Keep Away From The Castle.
You May Become A Prisoner.
Olivia.

Pages 126 & 127

You have to think back to '*THE ORDER OF THE JOUST*' on page 117. It says that the Black Knight is to joust against the Green Knight. As you are the '*Green Knight*' (for the moment at least!) your opponent must be the Black Knight.

Pages 128 & 129

There is a piece of paper in the treasury on page 128 which contains more information about the DRAGON. It talks of turning the '𝔇𝔯𝔞𝔤𝔬𝔫 against 𝔄𝔩𝔟𝔦𝔫' and letting 'it breathe its fire on him'. Baron Toadfettle obviously plans to try to use his DiRect Attack WaGON to kill the king! It is vitally important that his majesty learns this as soon as possible.

Pages 130 & 131

Those pretty fingernails should give you the vital clue. It's the Harlequin, whose fingernails match his diamond-patterned suit. You saw his ballad (and picture) on page 104. Be wary of trusting him — remember the words of that ballad!

Pages 132 & 133

There is a notice about the Room Without Locks in the Guardroom on page 120. The notice, headed '**REMINDER TO ALL PERSONNEL**', tells you that the Room Without Locks is 'at the top of the West Tower'.

Pages 134 & 135

The bag on page 135 is the give-away clue to the thief's identity. The pattern matches the suit of the Harlequin, a known trickster who will '*do anything for a bag of gold*'. In the Baron's Treasury on pages 128 & 129 the Portcullis Castle accounts state that the Harlequin has been paid one bag of gold — so must be working for Toadfettle. It looks as though he's been following

you, helping himself to items from around the castle as he went.

And you want to know where each item in the picture has come from? You'll have to find that out for yourself.

Pages 136 & 137

How many people are left on your list of possible prisoners? You may have more time than you bargained for to work out the solution . . .

The Solution

According to the letter from King Alvin on page 97, Baron Toadfettle "has either taken, or is about to take, one of my knights prisoner.". According to the papers in the evil Baron's chamber on pages 112 & 113, Toadfettle had narrowed it down to capturing one of four of the king's most trusted knights: Sir Flaxen, Sir Gareth, Sir Joan, or – believe it or not – you!

You know from the crumpled note on pages 118 & 119 that 'the Wanderer is still in foreign lands', and from pages 112 & 113 that the Wanderer is another name for Sir Flaxen. If Sir Flaxen is abroad, then he can't be the prisoner.

The letter on pages 124 confirms that Sir Gareth is also 'many months from the castle', so he can't be the prisoner, either.

And what of Sir Joan? Sadly, according to the 'order of joust', in the tent on pages 116 & 117, Sir Joan has 'died in battle', – which also makes this knight very unlikely to be the prisoner!

So who is the prisoner of Portcullis Castle? Why, you are, of course. That noise behind you, on pages 136 & 137, was the door slamming shut. That's the trouble with the Room Without Locks. It doesn't need them. According to a notice in the Guard Room on pages 120 & 121, the room has a 'sprung door that is easy to open from the outside but, once opened, automatically swings shut and stays shut. 'Tis not possible to open from within.' You walked into a trap. This was the important thing Haggard kept forgetting to tell you!

By leaking the story that he was about to seize one of the king's loyal followers, Baron Toadfettle was making sure that the king would send one of his most trusted knights to investigate . . . and that the investigator – who turned out to be you – would become the very prisoner you were sent to find!

You know from his conversation with Sir Clifford on pages 118 & 119 that the Baron was aware that the king's spy was in the castle. At the banquet, he was referring to you when he gave a toast, 'To King Alvin . . . and to his friend, a guest at Portcullis Castle!' though he didn't know, then, which of the king's loyal knights you actually were.

The Harlequin recognized you (from your photo on page 113) on pages 130 & 131, however, when you had your visor open and your undisguised face showing. He even said so. We know from the ballad in the minstrels' gallery, on pages 104 & 105, that the Harlequin would 'do anything for a bag of gold,' . . . and we can see from the accounts in the evil Baron's counting house, on pages 128 & 129, that Toadfettle has paid him that.

Once Harlequin knew who you were – a knight on Toadfettle's list and one the king himself described as 'one of my closest and most trusted knights', – he happily led you into the trap.

All is not lost

All the ingredients you need for a spell to escape from anywhere can – fortunately for you – be found in the Room Without Locks. All you need to do is remember the spell, follow the instructions and you should be free. Then you can warn King Alvin about the Baron's secret weapon, the 'DRAGON'.